A. J. Blay... (signature)

TWIN PULPITS

Papers of the Conference on
Church and Media in Modern Ireland
All Hallows College, July 1997

Edited by
Eamonn Conway & Colm Kilcoyne

GW00383152

VERITAS

First published 1997 by
Veritas Publications
7-8 Lower Abbey Street
Dublin 1

Copyright © The individual contributors, 1997

ISBN 1 85390 323 X

British Library Cataloguing
in Publication Data.
A catalogue record for
this book is available
from the British Library.

Cover design by Bill Bolger
Printed in the Republic of Ireland by Betaprint Ltd, Dublin

CONTENTS

PREFACE

'Not all the good guys are on one side, not all the bad guys are on the other. It was good to see both sides prepared to take criticism on the chin.' This was the comment of one participant at the conclusion of the 1997 All Hallows College Summer School on the media and the Churches.

All Hallows College hosted the conference in order to promote open, honest and frank discussion between two of the key players in the shaping of modern Ireland, media and Church, twin pulpits which in recent times have been largely at cross-purposes. Honest and frank discussion took place, and an environment was created in which the real issues emerged. This is not surprising given that both institutions, Church and media, are pledged to the service of truth.

Did the conference provide any grounds for hope? A number of participants commented on the professionalism of all who participated – journalists, broadcasters, Church spokespersons. Church people came to recognise that even where journalists are not themselves motivated specifically by religious conviction, they are anxious to be thoroughly professional in their reporting of Church news. It also emerged that the Churches have work to do in terms of communicating their message more efficiently. At the same time it was acknowledged that the Gospel does not easily convert into sound-bite.

What makes news 'news', the achievement of balance and fairness, ethics and standards in broadcasting, the critical role of media in Northern Ireland, the freedom and responsibility of Church-sponsored media, were all issues that surfaced in the course of the week. From the organisers' point of view what is significant is how readily media people seized the opportunity to discuss these matters in a Church setting. None of those who contributed had to be asked twice. This shows a concern on the part of media to understand the Churches better. It also shows that they still consider the Churches to be relevant and influential.

We extend our gratitude to all the contributors to the summer school, many of whose papers are published here.

Eamonn Conway
Colm Kilcoyne

20 September 1997

PART 1

CHURCH AND MEDIA: THEIR CONTRIBUTION TO SOCIETY

THE MEDIA AND THE CHRISTIAN CHURCHES

Dermot Mullane

I feel that I and some of those present are participating in what may well be a first. If I may be bold enough to equate those of us in the media with lions – in reality, of course, we are all the nicest kind of pussy cats – this might be the first occasion upon which the lions have been thrown to the Christians.

I am under no illusions. However well we in the media may believe we are doing our jobs, I do not expect a unanimous chorus of agreement from those, whether in the Christian Churches or elsewhere, upon whose day-to-day activities we are required to report and, indeed, lend some perspective.

The title given to this talk takes the form of an age-old question: 'What is news?' It is a very good question and one which, at considerable length, I am about to prove that I have no definitive answer. After nearly forty years in national journalism, first in a daily newspaper and for the past twenty-five years in the RTÉ News Division, I suspect the answer really is: anything you choose to regard as news.

A now retired senior news editor in the RTÉ News Division, when asked the question, always had a very simple and basic answer. 'News', he used to declare, 'is anything which the news editor decides is news.' Of course, there was a good measure of truth in his assertion. This morning, though, I will attempt to explain some of the criteria by which he and his successors came to that decision.

At its most basic, news may be the information conveyed over the garden fence by one neighbour to another that a much loved son or daughter is returning home for a holiday. On another level, it might be the announcement by a clergyman of deaths, altered times of Masses, services or meetings and other information of importance to the congregation.

For the purposes of this paper, I will define news as information of whatever kind that is regarded by professional journalists as 'newsworthy': in other words, of sufficient importance, significance or interest to merit its transmission to the wider public using the broadcast or print media.

Of course, it is important to point out that what is of interest is sometimes not significant and that what is significant or important, in terms of television, is not always interesting. Neither, though, should be excluded for that reason alone. Skilled journalism can make the intrinsically dull and unworthy into an item of interest: something in essence trivial can become significant if lent significance by the media. All that, of course, does not take us a whole lot further in trying to define news.

Let me add, or employ, other criteria. To be news, the matter must be something that, in essence, is informative. It must be relevant to the listeners or readers to whom it is addressed. Under the rules by which I am accustomed to operating, it must be presented accurately and fairly. And, of course, it has of its nature to be something of which those to whom it is addressed have not previously been aware. Yesterday's news, as we have all been told, is history.

At first sight, my assessment as a national public service news broadcaster of the newsworthiness of a given event may not have much in common with that of the editor of a mass circulation tabloid newspaper. However, I would assert that our approaches to newsworthiness, in essence, differ not a great deal. Both of us call upon a mixture of experience and received wisdom and, above all, both of us are governed by a knowledge of the audience or readership we serve.

Effectively, on any given day of the year there is available to all the news media an agenda or newslist of global and local events, some foreseen and others unforeseen. It can, to put it crudely, embrace events ranging from the opening of a night club to the result of a papal conclave, from the exposure of the sexual peccadilloes of a politician ... or even a member of the clergy ... to genocide in Rwanda.

It is what is done on the basis of that newslist that distinguishes one media outlet from another. And the choices that are made are conditioned by a whole range of factors: whether a newspaper is tabloid or broadsheet; whether it considers itself to be a newspaper of record or not; whether in the case of a radio or television station it regards news as a central and fundamental part of its operations or something to which it must pay mere lip service; whether it is public service in ethos or governed by sometimes crassly commercial and competitive considerations.

A host of other factors must be considered. Geographic location, the influence of proprietors, the structure of society, the literacy of the population, competition, the influence of Government upon media or Government perception of the role of media in a given society, are just some of the factors that may come into play.

As for public service broadcasters in the sense that most of us understand the term, it seems to me that we are frequently in the unenviable position of those who, in seeking to please everybody, end up by pleasing nobody. This, in itself, though, may be no bad thing. It is not our duty – and here I speak very much as one involved in public service news broadcasting – to promote specific policies, ideologies, economic or social theories.

If, as sometimes happens, those of opposing political, economic, religious or social views simultaneously voice criticisms of our journalism on the grounds that we are favouring the other side, it may just be because we've got things right and are favouring a balanced, middle-of-the-road approach rather than leaning in the direction which one or the other would favour. Not, of course, that any of our critics would ever concede a bias or partisan approach on their part.

There is a fundamental difference between the role of the public service broadcaster and that of other players on the contemporary media field in Ireland. RTÉ, I should point out, is obliged statutorily to express no editorial opinion. Section 18(1) of the Broadcasting Authority Act 1960, as amended, requires the RTÉ Authority to ensure that 'All news broadcast by it is reported and presented in an objective and impartial manner and without any expression of the Authority's own views'.

In this context, the broadcasting guidelines issued to RTÉ personnel define objectivity as the 'setting forth of an actual external situation, uncoloured by the feelings or subjective views of the broadcaster'. 'Impartiality' is defined as being seen to be fair and just in reporting and presenting the facts without favouring any particular interest or interests involved.

The same handbook has a lengthy section dealing with freedom of expression, which is grounded in large measure on Article 40 of the Constitution, as well as Article 10 of the 1948 Convention for the Protection of Human Rights and Fundamental Freedoms. It goes on to assert that as a corollary to the expressions contained in those documents, the communications media carry a serious duty in the provision of information.

It then asserts: 'As a foremost medium of communication and as a public service organisation, RTÉ accepts this responsibility in full. In doing so, it operates on behalf of the community as a whole.' This, I think, encapsulates the ethos that underpins the day-to-day activities of the RTÉ News Division. At all times we must seek to remember that we operate on behalf of the community as a whole. That community is as diverse as it is numerous. Self-evidently, we cannot satisfy all the strands of which it is composed all of the time. I can assert confidently that our failures, such as they are, are not failures bred of partiality or dishonesty.

In common with other media, RTÉ News also operates within a widely drawn legislative framework which, quite apart from the broadcasting legislation dealing specifically with its own operations, includes laws governing copyright, libel, contempt of court, privacy, official secrets, criminal procedure, the anonymity of complainants in rape and other cases dealing with sexual abuse.

I hope that by now the message that I am seeking to impart is becoming clear. RTÉ News operates within an environment calculated to ensure that, whatever individual viewers or listeners may allege, every effort is made to uphold accuracy, balance and fairness in its day-to-day activities.

Indeed, this sense of purpose is enshrined in RTÉ's own

internal guidelines for its news staff. In what might be described, to use contemporary jargon, as the News Division's 'mission statement', the section dealing with standards says:

> RTÉ News sets out to be accurate, truthful and objective, within the limitations of the law, which are fairly precise, and those of good taste and public morality, which can be subjective criteria. Controversy is covered. But RTÉ News has no editorial opinion. Space is limited – perhaps the equivalent of two or three columns of a newspaper – so the stories chosen for broadcast are mostly those which are adjudged to be important, significant and interesting. There are no precise limits: stories which are important and significant can sometimes be dull, while stories which are interesting can sometimes be slight or even trivial. Judgements on these matters are often value ones and vary from editorial person to person.

We have returned, I cannot but point out, to my original assertion that there is no precise definition of news. The best we can hope for, perhaps, is a general consensus, but within that consensus there is room for individual editors to differ in the amount of weight they attach to given events. This perhaps, if contained within reasonable limits, is to be welcomed as something that merely reflects the diversity of opinion among the population at large as to what constitutes news.

I turn again to our internal guidelines. I do so because I cannot over-emphasise the care which is taken, on a day-to-day basis, to ensure that our job as public service broadcasters is performed properly.

The news avoids being vulgar, sensational, or irresponsible. The unpleasant news generated by society (death, injury, distress, crime or horror, is not avoided, but is not broadcast in a morbid, titillating or irresponsible way. Regard is given to current social views on decency, propriety and morality, while maintaining the duty to inform about realities, sometimes painfully. This is, at times, a difficult path to negotiate, though the number of times that consensus is arrived at in these matters is, in itself, surprising.

In the broadcasting of news, thought is given to the dangers of distortion, particularly on film or videotape. Sometimes cameramen can only succeed in getting the fringes of a particular news story, but a far greater danger is being too close to the action: focusing on small sharp flashes of violence, for instance, and then having them presented, dramatically, out of context. Ten people, filmed enthusiastically and well, can create the appearance of a remarkable riot in a crowd of five hundred, or a thousand or more.

I will just quote a couple of further extracts from these internal guidelines for news staff.

It is no function of RTÉ to help create news, which a camera on location is sometimes capable of doing....

Apart from normal high standards of journalistic criteria, RTÉ is bound by the Broadcasting Acts to be fair and impartial in all news and current affairs broadcasts. This is particularly relevant in political matters....

Then, underlining a point I have made already:

> Further broadcasting limitations are there because the law says so....

> And finally there are rights of the person to his [the guidelines obviously should have added 'or her'] privacy, to his peace etc., rights which are not always protected by law but which are accepted in civilised societies.

Where does that leave us today as public service news broadcasters? The public service model upon which we in Ireland have drawn, for obvious reasons, has been that of our nearest neighbours. That model was largely the creation of Lord Reith who, a creature of his background, saw the BBC essentially as a vehicle for creating a better society imbued with, to contemporary eyes, fairly stern spiritual and moral values.

In a paper delivered some six-and-a-half years ago, my colleague and outgoing Director of News in RTÉ, Dr Joe Mulholland, quoted a declaration of the Church of England General Synod which asserted: 'The mainstream of opinion surely holds that the standards reflected in the programmes transmitted by a public controlled broadcasting service which is received in people's homes should be higher than the average of those found in contemporary society.'

'It is easy,' he commented, 'to dismiss these utterances as being stuffy and unrealistic, but the fact remains that the achievements of public service broadcasting have been and are considerable. Programme makers have to and do reflect moral, spiritual and human values in their work.' To that, I would add that news programmes on RTÉ radio and television news services on the whole, serve as a fairly accurate reflection of those values as they exist in Irish society as a whole.

On a daily basis and, indeed, from hour to hour for twenty-four hours a day and for three hundred and sixty-five days of the year, the news services of RTÉ hold up a mirror to society. There may be occasional and, I would argue, minor flaws in the mirror. Of far more significance when it comes to criticism of our output, it seems to me, is that some among us do not always like what we see when we look into the mirror. If the image is not that which we had hoped to see, human nature being what it is, we then tend to blame the mirror rather than ourselves. The result, too often, is a criticism of the broadcaster arising not from his or her actual failure, but from a perception of failure stemming from the bias, or prejudice, of the critic.

We are faced, at this point, with the old question of shooting the messenger if we don't like the message. Frequently, those who voice criticisms of the content or emphasis of news programmes do so from the perspective of what, to a dispassionate observer, must seem to be an innately biased view of their own.

Unlike RTÉ news personnel, who work within a well-defined legislative and organisationally regulated framework, designed as far as humanly possible to achieve fairness and balance in our reportage, these critics are subject to no such constraints.

I and my colleagues have no problem with criticism if it is fairly grounded. We do not claim that we always get things right. But we do seek to do so. And we do have a problem with criticisms which brook no expression of an opposite view to that of the critic, which bespeak an intolerance of other beliefs and ideas, which surely must be in marked contrast to the type of pluralist society that the Irish people, as a whole, publicly claim to espouse.

What, then, of our response to the activities of pressure groups? In this context, it has been suggested, not by me, that I might include the Churches. Pressure groups, espousing whatever cause, have a right not only to their views but to seek to have those views transmitted to as wide an audience as possible. In seeking that, they have a right to ask for the media's co-operation and assistance. However, they have no right to demand these.

Personally, I hesitate to include the Churches or, for example, the major political parties, employers' organisations, trade unions and other major bodies in Irish society under the category of pressure groups, although all of them, either as organisations or in the form of individuals or small groups from within them, can and do from time to time seek to exert pressure on us as public service news broadcasters.

It is our task, as far as we can, to assess the relevance of what they are saying, to contextualise it, to seek out balancing opinions or views, and then to decide whether we should report their views or otherwise. I do not claim that this is a perfect art. Obviously, as I have conceded already, subjectivity must from time to time creep into the day-to-day judgements of what constitutes the news of the day. I can and do claim that we do our best and that more often than not we get it right in large measure.

This does not mean that everybody who listens to or watches RTÉ radio and television news programmes is going to agree with either the content of those programmes or the priority accorded to individual stories within them. However, I do wish that from time to time our critics were more prepared to accept that we are professionals in our business, that our decisions are made professionally and that we not only operate in a fair and balanced manner but are obliged legislatively to do so.

As a long-serving television programme editor, responsible at various times for all our major television news programmes, I cannot begin to tell you how often I received complaints from individuals that they were bored with stories about the North. As an individual citizen, I too sometimes found myself bored – distressed might be a better word – with the seemingly never-ending stream of negative events and failed political initiatives of the last three decades. I would argue, though, that my individual feelings had no right to obtrude on the professional judgements which I made. The reality was, and remains, that the successful resolution, or otherwise, of the tragedy of Northern Ireland continues to exert a major influence on all our lives.

Talking to this audience, it would be remiss of me not to acknowledge that over the years the use of the word 'sectarian' to describe killings in the North has been the subject of frequent criticism from concerned members of all the major Churches. I understand their concern. I would point out, however, that when the openly expressed motivation of much of the violence is no more than the identification of the victim or target with a different religious denomination – and let us, perhaps shamefully, remember that all sides claim to be of the Christian faith – it is hard to avoid a proper use of the word 'sectarian'.

The leaders of all the principal Churches may condemn such actions in forthright terms. Indeed the vast majority of the members of those Churches may condemn them. The fact remains that the excuse for the violence is sectarian – albeit ineradicably linked to different political traditions – and to pretend otherwise would be an abdication of our professional responsibilities. The truth may sometimes be unpalatable, but it remains, none the less, the truth and, as we all learned as children, the truth can sometimes hurt.

I might add, while talking of the North, that we are criticised on an almost daily basis by extremists from both Republican and ultra-Unionist sides – not that they ever perceive themselves as carrying the slightest baggage or prejudice as critics. I picked up a telephone in the RTÉ newsroom the other day to be assailed aggressively by an angry woman asking why we had been so quick to assign responsibility for a particular bomb explosion to a particular Republican paramilitary group. This, she asserted, was another attempt to demonise them when everybody knew that it was, more likely, the work of Loyalist paramilitaries. The wind was taken somewhat from her sails when I explained that the reason for the attribution of responsibility was quite simple: the group concerned had claimed responsibility publicly.

Again let me sensibly concede that we do, being only human, sometimes get things wrong. Normally, when an error of significance has been confirmed, we seek to correct matters at the first available opportunity. Our errors are not errors of malice. More often than not, they arise from the effects of the great pressure that we confront – and that is not the pressure exerted by any person or group. It is the pressure – as a broadcaster, I would go further and say 'tyranny' – of time under which our daily activities are conducted. I hesitate to guess the number of individual decisions made during the preparation of a day's radio and television programmes. They are all made under extreme pressure of time. Any one of them made incorrectly can result in an error of fact or balance on air. The miracle, perhaps, is that we get so much right. And, if we don't? Well, there is always the threat of the Broadcasting Complaints Commission, which operates under powers conferred upon it by the Broadcasting Authority Act of 1960, as amended by the Broadcasting Authority (Amendment) Act of 1976.

So far as RTÉ News is concerned, the Complaints Commission can investigate and decide on complaints that 'in broadcasting a specified item of news, the Authority did not report and present it in an objective and impartial manner and without any expression of the Authority's own views, or failed to comply with prohibition to broadcast anything which might reasonably be regarded as being likely to promote, or incite to crime, or as tending to undermine the authority of the state'.

Not much room there, I would venture, for us to act irresponsibly as public service news broadcasters or to promote the individual viewpoints or agendas with which, if I were to listen to many of our critics, each one of us in the RTÉ News Division is associated.

Before I end, and I hope I have not gone on at too great a length, I will give you an illustration of how, in spite of all the care possible, things can go wrong – and I'm glad to say that it relates to my days as a newspaperman. Many of you will remember the time when the auxiliary bishops in the Roman Catholic Archdiocese of Dublin were given titular bishoprics and identified habitually by the media as the Bishop of Wherever.

One of those bishoprics was that of somewhere, I am not quite sure where it is located, called Nara. At that time, various towns were known officially by their Irish names:

Muine Bheag for Bagenalstown, Rathluirc for Charlesville, An Uaimh for Navan. Thus, the diligence of a team of sub-editors and printers in an Irish daily newspaper ensured that the Titular Bishop of Nara became first the Titular Bishop of Navan and, the full process of checks having been carried out, appeared in print as the Titular Bishop of An Uaimh.

I hope from all of this that you will have gathered that the words 'public service' are those which underpin in the most fundamental way the relationship of those of us privileged to work in RTÉ News with the public whom we serve. Our masters are the Irish people in all their diversity, and not any sectional interest. Our task must be accurately and fairly to represent the plurality and mores of the society in which we are founded. It is a task to which we remain committed on a daily basis.

No one, other than the Irish people as a whole, stands to benefit from the success of RTÉ and the news services which it provides; no one stands to lose, should they be diminished, other than the Irish people. That may sound a lofty assertion, but it is nothing other than the truth.

SPEAKING FOR THE CHURCHES

I

THE CHURCH AND THE MEDIA

Bishop Thomas Flynn

I have been asked to speak on 'How I see the role of the spokesperson for the Bishops' Conference in relation to the needs of the media'. This would not have been my choice of title if I had my way, but that decision has been made for me by the organisers of this summer school so I had better do what I have been told.

As I see it, the Church was the first medium with a mission for world-wide communications. Christ applied the words of Isaiah to himself: 'The Spirit of the Lord has been given to me for he has anointed me. He has sent me to bring the good news to the poor' (Luke 4:18). And he went from town to town preaching to the poorest – and frequently the most receptive.

His apostles followed his example, and in his apostolic exhortation on evangelisation in 1975 Pope Paul VI started with the sentence: 'the effort to proclaim the Gospel to the people of today, who are buoyed up by hope but at the same time oppressed by fear and distress, is a service rendered to the Christian community and to the whole of humanity'.

As the kernel and centre of his Good News, Christ proclaims salvation, this great gift of God which is liberation from everything that oppresses us, which is above all liberation from sin and the Evil One, in the joy of knowing God and being known by him, of seeing him and of being given over to him.

All this began during the life of Christ, but it must patiently be carried on during the course of history, in order to be realised fully on the day of the final coming of Christ, and that is the primary mission of the Church. It is in that context that she functions, whether in the media spotlight or out of it.

All baptised followers of Christ share the responsibility of proclaiming the message of salvation as a service to humanity. Bishops, priests, religious and, indeed, some lay people are full-time professionals in this mission, and as professionals who have devoted our lives to preaching the Gospel we must use all the media of communication at our disposal.

We do not discard the methods of the past – above all, the example of Christian living, prayer, the sacraments and preaching – but the Church must also use all the newer media now available to it.

In doing so we must be aware of the inherent dynamics of the media and the commercial pressures which a free-market economy place upon it. The news media, secular press, radio and television cater for a mass market and they concentrate on what is recent, vivid, entertaining or controversial, since these seem to be the criteria for success, i.e. high TAM ratings or larger readership than competitors.

The media are oriented to the here and now rather than the eternal, the visible rather than the invisible, the superficial rather than the profound, conflict rather than what unites, and for these reasons they tend to marginalise what principally concerns the Church.

In their need to be vivid and immediate, the modern media

simplify; they have very little place for deep reasoning. The noise of battle and controversy is perceived as having a wider viewing or listening audience.

Like it or not, this is the nature of the mass media. The Church, on the other hand, has to preach a Gospel, many of whose elements are intangible and reach to the depths of our being. Only their outward expression can find a niche in the mass media.

Big events like a papal visit or particular highlights in the Church's year, like Easter and Christmas ceremonies, are usually well covered in the media – the recent celebrations for the fourteenth centenary of Colum Cille's death is a prime example of how the media can focus on a religious theme.

But the media can and do also focus on human failure and abuse within the Church. We cannot object to this. Provided it is done in an objective and even-handed way it can be a cleansing experience, a reminder to us that we belong to a sinful race and that we owe our very existence as a Church to the fact that Christ came on earth to redeem this fallen world and reconcile it again with God.

But when it comes to the media, I wonder are journalists and producers expected to bracket out whatever religious convictions they may have in the interest of the all-important concept of balance?

Does the reader or the viewer always know from what standpoint an article or a programme has been written or produced for broadcasting, and in the absence of that knowledge aren't the less discerning put at a particular disadvantage? The viewer, the listener and the reader are better able to assess the neutrality or otherwise of a presentation if they know the background from which it comes and the loyalties or affiliation which underlie those who originate it.

We are all aware of the pressures under which the news media, in particular, must operate. There is first of all the factor of urgency – items have to be assembled in great haste and journalists often have to compose their stories in a matter of hours. This does not allow for in-depth analysis or detailed research. This is a need for which the Irish bishops made provision when they set up the Catholic Press and Information Office more than twenty years ago.

The bishops are now conscious of the media's need for a more immediate response from them on issues as they arise. They are also aware of the ever-developing use made of the technology of communication, such as the Internet. We are in the process of setting up a response to these needs and of making the teachings of the Catholic Church more accessible.

But I believe the media cannot disclaim responsibility for not employing people with adequate theological formation or expertise to assess correctly developments within the Church and their impact on society. In the past it could be argued that lay graduates were not available, but that is no longer the case. There are several third-level colleges offering theology to degree and doctorate level and there are now many graduates.

We should expect a high level of competence from our religious affairs correspondents and commentators. I do not say this to disparage any of our present correspondents. I am simply suggesting that in future this should be considered a qualification for appointment to such important positions.

I am happy to say that as Catholic Church spokesperson I have never experienced hostility from any section of the Irish media and if I did have any complaint it was that the media's perception of what was important was different from mine. I do remember one bishop going to a lot of trouble to brief himself for an interview – he was no novice to the media –

and in his judgement he did a very good interview, but the only sentence which was quoted was an *obiter dictum,* an offhand comment that had no bearing on the subject of the interview.

It is perfectly understandable that interviews may have been shortened to accommodate the limitations of the media, but we must also raise the question of the ideological outlook of an editor or programmer. This can slant a programme in a particular way and the balance which we all seek may be undermined.

What do we mean by 'balance'? Does it mean, for instance, that when the Pope speaks for the Catholic Church some contradictory voice must be found straight away to disagree with him in order to achieve balance? If this were to become the norm it would reflect a media devoid of all values, rather than one which is open to all. If this reflects the culture in which we live, perhaps we should all start to sit up and take notice. The Churches, especially all the Christian Churches, should seek to highlight those values that unite us rather than those that divide. Recently we have seen how a united approach on the Education Bill by the main Church bodies in the Republic worked for the benefit of all.

One of the greatest challenges facing us all today is a word culture eating into our own inherited culture. This need not be a bad thing, provided we can hold on to our Christian values and help mould the new culture rather than allow it to take us over without our involvement or consent.

The encounter with a plurality of cultures, while always a factor in human history, has been multiplied and intensified by our global mass media. We can react to this in different ways: either we can retreat into the security of an inherited conservatism or we can abandon all that made us what we are. Or we can become active in the building of a new culture in which our Christian values are preserved.

The first of these reactions is called conservative, and the second is called liberal. The third would occupy the middle ground but it does not conform to the modern media's perception of the unbending conservative or the radical liberal. The middle ground is characterised by subtleties of language which cannot be expressed in a thirty-second sound-bite on the evening news.

We have no doubt about the value and importance of the Church's teaching. This is our responsibility and I would appeal to professionals in the media to help make what is important equally interesting and audience-friendly.

I would also ask professionals in the media to consider the importance of sensitivity. I appreciate that we all fail in this regard from time to time, but we should try to balance what we say, write or present in graphic form about another person in such a way as we would if the victim or offender were a member of our own family. In this way we would never demonise or dehumanise any person. There is no one, however great his or her crime may be, who is beyond redemption.

As a final word, could I appeal for the return of that good old virtue of forgiveness. After all, God does not judge us before the end of our days, and in today's culture of hatred and revenge a forgiving world could help calm the anger that envelopes us and facilitate a happier world for us all.

II

CHURCH AND THE MEDIA: SERVANTS, NOT FRIENDS?

Liz Gibson Harries

'Nobody is on my side, nobody takes part with me: I am cruelly used, nobody feels for my poor nerves.'

Jane Austen, *Pride and Prejudice*

When I started my job as Church of Ireland Press Officer eleven years ago, someone said to me 'I hope you have a strong faith, you will need it'. I thought this was a very pessimistic view, but I have come back to the thought over and over during my time in the Press Office.

As press officers we are required to translate Church news to the general public via the media and to publicise the Church's work, to extend the kingdom of God. Today, we have many ways open to us to do this – newsprint, radio, television, video and, more recently, the Internet – and we would be failing in our duty if we didn't address all of these potential channels with vigour and integrity. Historically the Churches have shied away from what we collectively call 'the media' for two main reasons in my view. Firstly, that it wasn't the 'done thing' to appear in the press to publicise one tradition to the detriment of another, and anyway if you were in the press it was probably for the wrong reasons.

Secondly, for the very reason that I address this meeting, because the media were not seen as friends, and that anything you said to a journalist would be misconstrued, turned around, and what you said, or meant to say, would be misrepresented. Coming from a background in journalism, although closer to the soil – in equestrianism – than heaven, I have, I think, the mind and the nose of a journalist. I'm the poacher turned gamekeeper, as it were. I began, as all journalists should, in local papers and broadcasting, being given the job of reading the news because I could pronounce the names of Russian leaders. I covered local sewer rows and baby shows. I broke a canoeing doping story and covered the 1976 Olympic Games in Montreal – so I think I can tell when a story is worth a press release.

Over the years I have admired writers and broadcasters such as Mark Tully and our own Fergal Keane, whom I first met in RTÉ, then in the BBC and subsequently in South Africa just before he left. Such journalists inspire integrity in others, portraying what they see with eloquence and honesty, painting pictures in the listeners' minds, unafraid to challenge common beliefs, and it is these attributes that we require in the press at this time. I have found that 'off the record' briefings with journalists before a General Synod or at the height of a story can often minimise the impact by supplying a background, but there has to be the element of trust between us for this system to work.

It is common knowledge that the media does not simply reflect the attitudes of society but helps to form them. It therefore follows that journalists potentially hold a great deal of power and responsibility. RTÉ, in the form of Gay Byrne, did a great deal for the people of the Republic of Ireland, of every denomination, especially in rural areas, to highlight some of the more taboo sexual subjects – abortion, contraception and incest. The fact that people could express their feelings without being identified – by means of the phone-in – was of enormous service to the community.

Likewise, the *Talkback* programme on BBC Northern Ireland, fronted by David Dunseath, has allowed frustration to be voiced. Some of it, one has to say, is bitter and fundamentalist, but in a democracy everyone is free to express their views. The Church of Ireland has a compelling adherence to the continuation of public service broadcasting on all the national systems. Religion is part and parcel of society in Ireland and should be seen as such by the broadcasters, not only in well-made religious-type programmes such as the UTV, and soon to be RTÉ programme *Crossing Borders,* in which a Presbyterian minister quizzes Protestants in the Republic about their life as a minority. This series is unlocking some of the preconceived ideas about life in the Republic for Northerners who have not or will not cross the border, and is a valuable aid to greater understanding.

All right-thinking people are urging greater communication to find out what the hopes and fears of both traditions are. Politicians have to safeguard their positions, but others are free to explore greater links with each other, and the media can and do assist greatly in this.

We need to support our national media against the threat from the Murdochs of this world, where one powerful man owns and manipulates an empire of media outlets, and also from satellite-projected programmes, emanating outside our jurisdiction and alien to our sense of decency. We see the dangers of the Internet, but that doesn't mean we have to back away from its use.

Thankfully, most of the Churches have decided to engage professional and full-time press officers not only to translate Church news, but to explain the media to the Churches, to select and train spokespersons on specific subjects and to prepare them for emergencies and the requirements of today's media.

At a summer school I attended some years ago in Mayo the principal speakers were two of the most high-profile press officers of our recent times – P. J. Mara, Taoiseach Haughey's press officer, and Bernard Ingham, Prime Minister Thatcher's press officer. During a question-and-answer session, I asked both how far they would go to protect their bosses. One replied, if my boss said 'jump' I would ask not how high but how far, and the other laughed and said as far as it takes. I won't betray who said what.

The media lay great demands on the Church press officers to deliver; to get up-to-date, factual news and a quote or spokesperson, within a very short time-scale. I have always been of the opinion that the public expect the Churches, of all institutions, to be open and honest, and I will not be party to any cover-ups, but will be as honest with a journalist as I possibly can. The 'media' in Ireland, North and South, are mostly not as aggressive or intrusive as the British media, which leads us to enter into good relations with the journalists we deal with regularly. I'm not sure the media or the Churches should be the servants of each other; as in all walks of life, trust is necessary on both sides. Trust that the truth (or most of it) will be told and that it will be reported without a slant, spin or prejudice on the part of the journalist.

The Churches are made up of human beings – the clergy come from the laity originally, and the fact that we raise the clergy up on pedestals makes it hard for some of them to live up to expectations. If that is so, regret and forgiveness must be meted out. The news media is a hungry animal, and what makes news and looks like the end of the world at 11 p.m. could well have become old news in twenty-four hours if the truth is told. Another unfortunate thing I have learned by bitter experience is that nothing is really as black as it looks.

I have the privilege of serving the Church of Ireland on both sides of the border and, apart from the violence, the concerns and certainly the attitudes are different North and South. The Church of Ireland has a total of forty-seven women in the ministry at present. When General Synod agreed to their ordination and, incidentally, not inflicting the glass ceiling which would ban them from becoming bishops in God's good time, the media had a field day. We moved to this decision before the Church of England, Scotland or Wales, so there was great interest, but working with the women I was impressed by their dignity; no triumphalism, no overt signs of disregard for others' feelings and beliefs, and although some journalists wanted to portray them as second-rate men, as oddities and curiosities, I believe the ordination of these women over seven years has become of little or no news value and that's how it should be. They have impressed me that they have the same calling as men, and their gender should be no bar.

I suppose the most difficult issue I have had to deal with, and it will come as no surprise to you, is a press officer's nightmare – Drumcree. The ramifications have gone around the world and are continuing to do so. It is my ideal not to be political in this address, but unfortunately religion and politics are so tightly interwoven in Ireland that it is almost impossible to divide them at times. Within our own Church we are looking at any words or deeds that would seem to be sectarian. The media has been both friend and foe in this issue. Since 1995 sectarianism has been eating away at communities as never before, clergy of all denominations are in the middle of all this, and so often journalists desire interviews or comment from Church leaders and church-goers over incidents such as attacks on people or property. Over the years I have wrestled with myself to find new words of condemnation and regret. Words sound so hollow and empty in times of sorrow. The role of the press officer must always be to reflect the mood of his or her Church, not to voice a personal opinion, and over the last eleven years that has been extremely trying and taxing for me.

Where a serious press enquiry demands a serious reply, there have been times when one would doubt the sanity of the enquirer. I wouldn't say I welcome telephone calls in the small hours or on Christmas Day, but I will deal with them if they are (1) relevant, and (2) genuinely urgent, but to be asked early on a Sunday morning for directions to a church service or the Christian name of an interviewee two weeks ahead of publication, can try the patience of a press officer just too far! At times like that it is hard to be civil and to remember the person on the other end of the phone is another human being with a job to do!

A great deal of the time and energy of any press officer is taken up in briefing. In today's secular society, many journalists have no specialist knowledge of a religious dimension. Clergy are indignant when their titles are incorrect, and so often we have to assume that the enquirer has no basic knowledge of Churches at all. This area must have hit rock bottom for a colleague of mine in the Methodist Press Office in London, when an American journalist demanded an interview with John Wesley!

We also have to take the brunt of criticism from our own side of what the Church and its leaders say and do. When I write my autobiography it will be called *I want to speak to Mr Eames* – I know I'm in trouble when I get those sort of calls!

It is said of a senior British politician that when asked to confront the enemy opposite he replied 'Gentlemen, the enemy is behind me'. So often we – the press officers – have to run the gauntlet of some of our own denomination; this is never more true than at times of sectarian attacks, when the Church is expected to represent its own 'tribe'. The saddest thing of all is that the message of Jesus to love thine enemy, is so hard today with historical baggage and the tit-for-tat attitude of some people. The Kingdom of Heaven seems too far away and too hard to find when tempers are flared and jibes and taunts fill the air.

But over the last eleven years, I have had to pay tribute to the main body of journalists in Ireland, especially the religious affairs correspondents of *The Irish Times, The Irish Independent,* RTÉ, *The Irish News* and *The Belfast Telegraph* and *Newsletter* for their patience and understanding. There have, of course, been times when we have clashed, you wouldn't expect otherwise, but I think it's true to say that relations between the Churches and the media have never been better, both realising that the other has a job to do. Having said that, I do believe that the media carries a heavy responsibility. Headlines and photographs are what people remember, and I beg of them all to be a responsible part of their own community. Foreign media do not have to live with the situation all year. They are here for the sensational and they speak only to the fundamental activists on both sides. No one, it seems, wants to hear our good stories of reconciliation and appeals for justice. On trying to promote the opening of a church premises for profoundly handicapped people, I couldn't believe my ears when a reporter asked me if there would be a row, thereby making a story out of it!

My colleagues in Britain and America cannot believe that

the Churches here get so many column inches and so many media enquiries. Either the press officers are getting it right or we are what we claim the Churches ought to be – an integrated part of society. I often wonder what would take the place of the Churches if the begrudgers have it right and the Churches lose their constituents. Society needs a watchdog and that is down to the Churches in the final analysis: What is right or wrong? How far can you push medical research or vengeance in the law? Society is changing and so must the Churches, not in their basic belief in the love and forgiveness of Christ, but in their attitudes and practices – to be with people who hurt and have fallen.

Society must have a press – it brought us news of famine in Africa, students' plight in China, kidnapping in Beirut and wonderful things like the end of apartheid and the Spice Girls – but if it becomes neither a servant nor a friend, then it could become a force for small-mindedness, invasion of privacy and suspicion, all things that the Churches stand opposed to. As we approach the millennium, the celebration of two thousand years of Christianity, when people will be joining religious sects, jumping off high buildings or experimenting with older beliefs, it would be refreshing if the media, with whom I work and have a high regard, would for once believe in the message of our founder 'Peace I leave with you – my peace I give you' (Jn 14:27).

I am rather reluctant to single out the issue of Drumcree and the marching season in Northern Ireland. I realise, of course, that it is of particular interest to the media and to the public in general at this time of year, but it is only a part of my job and has only been so for the last three years. Hopefully, it will not feature so highly in future years.

No matter where you go in the world, no matter what

language is spoken, the picture of the parish church of Drumcree portrays not only the 1995 and 1996 stand-offs, but any other marching disturbance. *The Sunday Times* in May had a whole page on the dispute at Dromore, with a half picture of Drumcree – the building has come to symbolise the clash between marchers and residents' groups anywhere in the Province. Any conversation between Northerners and Southerners – since Drumcree – tends to end up by talking of the next Drumcree. Although the Church of Ireland parish church is where the Orangemen come traditionally to a morning service of worship, it is not an Orange service. For many years it passed off peacefully, but since the Orangemen were prevented from leaving the surrounding area and spent some days in the churchyard and parish hall, it has gained some notoriety. There are dozens of other Protestant churches in Northern Ireland where the Orangemen attend worship and they have never been heard of. It is not for me to say whether marching to worship is right or wrong. Certainly the worship of Almighty God is right, so long as it is not used in a sectarian way; violence should not follow. In the Church of Ireland no bishop has the authority to ban services; it is up to the rector and the select vestry to make those decisions.

In this case, as Church of Ireland Press Officer, I am helpless to 'deal' with the media as such. This year I have got agreement that I have the authority not to allow the media into the church, and as with the many years of terrorist-related funerals, I have no jurisdiction over the media once off the church property. I realise the media have a job to do, but I have a duty to protect the Church of Ireland from the scenes inside the church that would send the wrong signals to the public.

Like it or not, Northern Ireland, the conflict, politics and sectarianism, take up a great deal of my time – and life. Eleven years ago, when I was appointed, I was living in County Wicklow, but was moved North due to the 'bulk of news being in Northern Ireland'.

During the time before the ceasefires in 1994 I was never far from a radio, day or night. I began listening to the BBC World Service all night, a practice I still continue. I have trained myself to waken at 3 and 5 a.m., roused by Lilly Bolaro, to hear the news, to be prepared for any attack which took place overnight. If an attack, on either community, or by either group of paramilitaries had taken place, the procedure would go thus:

> Ring Police/Army press officer. Ask only for denomination of victim (names are generally not released until all relatives have been informed). Call the bishop of the diocese and the clergy. Obtain the information, arrange interviews and spokespersons. Issue condemnation and/or appeal for calm. Prepare for funeral – where , when, who is conducting the funeral or preaching? Does the family want privacy? etc.

Early on I made the decision, unless families decided otherwise, not to allow cameras into the churches. Private grief should be allowed to be just that – private. I also very actively discouraged camera operators from running alongside widows and children during processions and certainly on church property. The home media were always co-operative, the 'blow-ins' not so.

During the commemorations of twenty years of the arrival of the first British troops on the streets, German TV crews were discovered supplying children with toy guns and balaclavas to set up shots. The home media ran them for giving the whole industry a bad name.

Unfortunately some mornings the feeling was – thank goodness, only one person killed. What kind of person had I become, thanking God for an acceptable level of violence?

My memories include the awful sound of 'Abide with me' being played at slow-march pace through country lanes preceding coffins and weeping families; tiny picturesque country churches surrounded by fields of grazing animals and peaceful pastures, with the solemn bell tolling every two minutes; one tiny cottage where a coffin had to be brought through the front door standing up, as there was no room to turn it in the doorway.

I know it took its toll on journalists too – no chance for covering 'good news' stories, only coverage and reaction of bitterness and violence. After the ceasefires it became obvious that newsrooms were almost unable to do 'normal' stories.

As far back as the late 1980s Archbishop Eames and Cardinal Ó Fiaich asked the Ballymascanlon meetings to study sectarianism, and a booklet was produced. However, you cannot legislate for reconciliation and understanding, and anyway I believe that the two communities are light years away from reconciliation. A basic acknowledgement of each other's traditions and rights and a freedom from the threat of violence for a sustained period is the best we can hope for at present.

RELIGION AND MEDIA: A NATIONAL EDITOR'S OUTLOOK

Matt Cooper

I feel qualified to speak only about the newspaper for which I have responsibility, not the rest of the media. *The Sunday Tribune,* as I saw it before I joined it, and as I have tried to maintain it, while changing certain elements of its content, is what I would see as a liberal newspaper, respectful of the rights and views of all its readers, not just Catholics, but believing in a fair and inclusive society for all Irish citizens and all those who live within its shores, writing, among other things, reports about issues in Irish life which cause division and inequality, and hoping that this will lead to something being done about it by those who have the power to do so.

I think *The Sunday Tribune* has a fine tradition of sticking up for the marginalised and disadvantaged in society, writing the reports which other newspapers may not regard as important or popular. I would hope that we do not merely pander to the views and aspirations of the more well-off and advantaged sections of society, or those who have traditionally exercised power and have influenced the media in what they have told people about the workings of Irish society.

Perhaps in doing so we are somewhat anti-establishment, but then I believe that a good newspaper should always be questioning and probing those in positions of power, responsibility and authority on behalf of the underdog.

Archbishop Connell of Dublin has said that 'it is not surprising that there should be a close correspondence between the law of the land and Catholic moral teaching in respect of a host of crimes from tax evasion to rape. Such crimes are forbidden by the law, not because Catholic teaching rejects them but because they injure the common good. It is clear that no vision of the common good is possible if it is not a moral vision as well'.

But is he suggesting that somehow non-Catholics in the legislature and media do not have moral values which inform their views on issues like tax evasion and rape? In the same sermon he spoke of the difficulties that teachers and parents were facing because of a variety of pressures, 'not least the influence of media support for a materialistic and permissive vision of life, not to speak of their hostility towards Catholic standards'.

Archbishop Dermot Clifford of Cashel and Emly, speaking prior to the 1986 divorce referendum, warned that if the 'national media continued their bombardment of secular, liberal and pagan ideas, then we shall be forced to assert ourselves a little and become protagonists of Christian values, as Pope John Paul II put it'.

Perhaps the damage done by the scandals has made the media less responsive to the interesting, sometimes socially progressive statements made by members of the hierarchy.

Many of the people who complain most that the media does not adequately reflect the real will of the people are those who garnered so few votes in the latest general election. The National Party and the Christian Solidarity Party, in constituencies where they ran high-profile candidates, received fewer votes than the television deflector candidate who was elected to the Dáil for Donegal South.

Global mass communications and travel are changing our attitudes. Archbishop Desmond Connell is one of the people most worried by this and, from reading many of the articles which outlined his comments, it appears he blames the media for many things.

He has spoken about a revolution in values. He says that Ireland has undergone profound change in the last twenty years, which in other industrialised European countries had taken nearly 150 years to happen. He has spoken of the intrusion of the mass media, the impact of mass global tourism, the communications explosion, unemployment or fear of losing a job, divorce, all things which affect and haunt many families today. Not all families are pressured to the same degree, but some are damaged by forces beyond their control.

But what about the flip-side? That life is so much better for many people than it was before; that the other countries which experienced change may not be any less well-off for it, but may actually have seen the quality of their life enhanced. It is legitimate for the media to point all of this out.

Dr Connell has also criticised the 'increasing influence of permissive propaganda' in the legislature and the media, which he said is 'testing not only our young people but the strength of our family tradition'.

Does the Church perhaps blame the media for its own problems in relating to its flock rather than analysing its own position?

Was the media wrong in its hounding of Bishop Comiskey? Perhaps it was. But perhaps the Church was also wrong in how it handled the problem.

Perhaps the Church should be delighted that the media cares so much, that it demands the same standards of religious leaders as it does of its political and business leaders, for example.

The Catholic Church got it soft for too long – its comments and statements were reported but not analysed or commented upon. Now the Church is treated more like other bodies, in that it is entitled to say what it believes about social referenda, but equally newspapers are entitled to point out that the Constitution is meant to serve all the people of this nation, Catholic, Protestant or dissenter.

Newspapers are entitled to hold the belief that while the Church can instruct its members to vote in referenda in a certain way, in an attempt to ensure that the Constitution or legislation suits the Catholic Church, newspapers are also entitled to point out that it is deeply unfair to the people not of the Catholic Church whose rights are every bit as important. It is important for sections of the media to point this out if they so want.

Some people say the newspapers should reflect the Catholic will of the people. Well, those people can set up their own newspaper and let market forces decide.

The Church has a voice, like any other, which should be facilitated by the media, but it must also be analysed and criticised.

I have no difficulty in letting the Church have its say. Too often, perhaps, it is shy in doing so, or selective in choosing the outlets to which it wants to present its message.

I think the role of the Christian Brothers in providing education has been well documented and acknowledged by the media. But I can speak from personal experience of a rather vicious, violent culture which prevailed in the Christian Brothers' school which I attended during the late 1970s and early 1980s. Brothers took advantage of the fact that such incidents were rarely spoken about, that parents in many cases did not believe their children, or that children did not know what was happening and did not tell their parents, because the media had never highlighted what was happening. It was only, I believe, when some stories started appearing in the newspapers that others realised that what had happened to them, or was happening to them, was wrong, and reacted to it.

For too long the media was remiss in reporting what people knew was happening. The Church cannot complain when the media finally starts doing its duty. It is natural in those circumstances that once the floodgates open, so to speak, many other people come forward with tales to tell. The media cannot ignore that, or pretend it did not happen. It most definitely should not suppress such reports just because it may cause image problems for the Catholic Church.

Father Stephen Rossetti, the American priest who is an expert on clerical child sex abuse, and who was brought to Ireland to assist in dealing with the problem, was right to state that 'it is not constructive to judge past ineffective Church and Government responses to sexual abuse by current standards'.

Rossetti also said the media ought to continue to raise public awareness of this cancerous societal secret. 'Child sexual abuse has been a lightning rod for centuries of buried resentment and anger towards the Catholic Church in Ireland. My fear is that this anger will blind many to the human beings in today's Church who are trying to respond to the problem despite their own discouragement and pain.'

Cardinal Daly acknowledged that soul-searching is required by the Church in terms of how it regards the media. 'Too often,' he said, 'our attitudes are defensive and suspicious'. Yes, I believe there is a lot of 'shooting the messenger' involved. You have to remember that the media, as well as ordinary citizens, have been lectured for many years about standards of morality which must be adhered to, yet here were those prominent in giving lectures who were not pure and chaste themselves.

In relation to investigations of child sexual abuse Daly made the very important point that many questions should be asked about the level of state funding for child-rearing institutions at the relevant time; the quality of state child-care and support services; the availability of child-care training courses; the state of the psychological and social work services; the level of awareness of child psychology in Ireland at the time; the support offered by various Government departments.

Cardinal Daly was right to defend the Orders and he will have found that his defence was reported in detail at the time.

The Church indeed did take up the slack left by the state, a state which failed to fulfil its basic functions and left the work to the Church. The Church has done powerful good over the years, but unfortunately a number of individuals took advantage of their position to abuse children and this has tarnished all of the other good work. But just as due recognition of the good work should not be ignored, it is impossible to forget about the shortcomings and it would be irresponsible for the media to ignore them just because some people fear it will do damage to the image of the Church.

What is unusual or sensational is what gets major news coverage because that is what people are interested in. People who complain about media coverage of child sex abuse scandals, for example, often refuse to believe the evidence presented or just wish that it would go away. What they effectively require of the media is suppression of the facts, and no newspaper can do that. That, I believe, is what critics of the media often want.

The managing editor of the *Irish Catholic,* Otto Herscham, claimed in 1995 that 'today the Church in Ireland is forever on the defensive, or perhaps it would be more accurate to say the bishops are. The media have very consciously created a war situation'. He also told the bishops to 'desist from excusing their actions or their inactivity' in response to the media and to concentrate on their 'teaching role'.

What nonsense. Perhaps there are some journalists who have worked to a secret agenda to highlight these issues so as to weaken the position of the Church in the run-up to referenda. But I doubt it.

Last year, Cardinal Daly asked editors, producers and journalists to examine to what extent the ethics of journalism, requiring fairness, balance and integrity, may have been transgressed. I believe that the majority of journalists adhere to those standards, and if they don't, their editors ensure that nothing gets into the public domain which does not adhere to those standards.

Separately, Cardinal Daly has also complained about the 'relentless and pitiless pursuit' by some media of 'recent scandals', 'where fact often jostles with innuendo and insinuation, hint and suggestion [which], especially where the dead or absent are concerned, is obsessive, some would say malicious'.

I am not aware of any anti-Church campaign in the media or parts of it. It may be that a lot of journalists do not regularly attend religious services, but a lot of them do, and in that regard journalists are much like many other sectors of Irish society.

It has been difficult for the Church in this decade, with the controversies regarding Bishops Eamon Casey and Brendan Comiskey, Father Michael Cleary and various child sex abuse cases.

Ask yourself what you would have done if you were editing a newspaper when any of the stories started running.

Who could, or should, have ignored the Eamon Casey affair...?

Some of the Bishop Comiskey coverage was lurid, grossly intrusive and repetitive, to use the words chosen by Father Kevin Hegarty in an article he wrote for *The Irish Times*. But Comiskey had major questions to answer in relation to his handling of child sex abuse allegations at Monageer, and his fitness to hold his position also became a relevant issue.

There were problems with Goldenbridge and I believe the Sisters of Mercy have tried to respond in an honest and open manner.

In relation to Michael Cleary, human weakness in members of the clergy would be accepted if those same individuals were not preaching to the laity about their own moral standards.

Whether the space given to these scandals in the newspapers was disproportionate or not is a matter of opinion. I do not believe that it was, although there may have been times, because of the lack of corroboration offered by the authorities, when newspapers and other media went too far.

As well as being a statement of intent and aspiration, and proffering a definition of editorial realities, what I've said up to now is also a marketing statement. While believing in those aspirations we journalists do what we think will help to sell newspapers. This would apply to most newspaper editors, whose central target is to sell newspapers while also creating a product which they can hold up with a certain level of pride, because they know that it is worthwhile. But what goes into those newspapers is what sells them. So as well as including all of the things which editors and journalists believe the readers should be interested in, we also have to include what the readers want, or we will not sell sufficient newspapers to justify our existence.

A bit clinical? Perhaps. But don't get the impression that this means a lowering of standards, a desire to go down the tabloid route, as some people would imply. Indeed, I believe that certain newspapers, like *The Sunday Tribune,* only succeed by attempting to uphold the highest standards. We may not always succeed but we have standards and morals and a belief in the way Irish society should be. That may not coincide with the teachings of the Catholic Church, particularly on issues like divorce, but it does not mean that we are in any way less moral.

In researching this paper, through reading many articles carried in the national media this decade, I have been tempted to come to the conclusion that many high-ranking clerics believe the media are not only a godless lot, with no morals or sense of right or wrong, but are also engaged in a conspiracy to undermine the belief of people in the Catholic Church in Ireland. Not only are we trying to damage the Church but we are doing so as a stepping stone to the introduction of a deeply permissive and immoral society.

Well, as it happens, we do not sit in committee dreaming up ways of how to undo the Catholic Church. Far from it. Indeed *The Sunday Tribune* may have succeeded as a newspaper in its eighteen years of existence because it was a new voice for a modern Ireland, although there would be others who may suggest that it has struggled because the voice it offered was not a popular one with the majority of people. But we continue to do what we think is right.

The media do omit important items. At a Famine Commemoration Mass Cardinal Daly made some highly interesting observations about the role of the rich capitalist nations of the world, including Ireland, and their unjust economic policies. Andy Pollak of *The Irish Times* noted that this 'harsh and prophetic indictment of our economic system by the moral leader of the vast majority of the nation's people was all but ignored by both the national broadcaster and the state's largest selling newspaper'.

I do not believe that journalistic standards are slipping. I do not believe there is less concern for accuracy, and the so-called feeding frenzy, where all the media descend on the one story, is nothing more than competition. There is honesty, fairness and balance in most of what is written in the newspapers; it is often when those qualities are most in evidence that people complain the most, because it is not the public relations spin that is being printed.

Notwithstanding that, such accusations are insulting to the many journalists who are religious, and are all tarred with the one brush, and to the many other journalists who are not religious but operate to high personal moral standards. There is a criticism that says the Catholic Church has become too reluctant to argue its point. But that is not the fault of the media.

In a speech in early 1995 the Progressive Democrats' leader Mary Harney said that the Catholic Church's capacity for 'dogmatic intervention in social and legislative matters was significantly undermined by Bishop Casey's misfortunes and the spate of clerical child abuse cases'. She maintained that a sense of fragmentation and introspection within the Church itself had contributed to the decline.

At the same conference Professor Dermot Keogh stated that 'some elements in the Catholic Church and among lay people would favour a return of the comfortable relationship which existed between Church and state before the 1960s. A rekindling of such a relationship would be neither desirable or possible'. I agree.

PART 2

CHURCH AND MEDIA: SERVANTS OR FRIENDS?

COMMUNICATION FOR COMMUNION

Helena O'Donoghue RSM

My intention is to refer to a few key dynamics which I think colour the interaction of our two bodies, particularly when the Church is on the mat, so to speak. There is usually a general clamour for a forthcoming and outspoken Church in such situations, and the Church often runs for cover! Some of these dynamics also apply when the Church wishes to speak out on some social issue or other. A silent Church is then the preferred option, raising the old chestnuts of separation of Church and state and the civil right to speak. However, the latter situation is for another session of your seminar. I hope that what I have to say may be helpful and relevant to our discussions on the former, as I will be arguing for a more communicating Church, whatever the situation.

Setting the scene

Before dealing with these dynamics I would like to set a basic scene. It is no exaggeration to say that Church is in a low popularity mode for some time now. It is fashionable and acceptable to be anti-Church. One way of looking at this is to see it in a historical perspective. The post-Famine Church grew from strength to strength for over one hundred years. It had reorganised and gained enormous power and status by the time of independence early in this century. For the next fifty years it worked closely with and exercised great influence on the state – seen as a Catholic state – and with whatever party was in power. All this was done with the agreement of the people at the time in the interests of 'salvation' and the good of the human endeavour. The Church did not see anything wrong with this situation and did not see any need for change. We are, of course, referring to another time, a time very different from today.

In the context of change and upheaval I believe that we as Church cannot be ambiguous about our basic *raison d'être*. Communication is of the very nature of the Church. The founder is the very WORD. The task of the Church is to share the Word of God – a word of hope, a word of challenge, a word of compassion, a word of healing, a word of forgiveness, a 'Word made flesh' in the humanity of Jesus Christ. As members of the Church he founded, as disciples, we are called to grow into the capacity to speak the word of life in all situations. Each of us fails many times in life; as a body we fail many times in life. These failures have to be addressed, challenged, highlighted so that our word may become more authentic. Yet in the end we cannot but speak, unless we are to deny our *raison d'être*.

Media play a valid and important role in questioning and searching the Church's word, and in fact have done us a service in highlighting abuses of trust. This is legitimate and we need to be open to it. But our failures do not free us from the obligation to do better the next time, nor does a damaged credibility negate our right to speak the word of hope tomorrow. It is a false notion of human life to see in absolute terms the profile of any organisation. By whatever philosophical terms you understand it, faithfulness to one's standards and aspirations, whether on an individual or corporate level, is not achieved easily or without many set-backs on the way. Grace and growth and commitment are required. If the media sets itself up (and I believe it has) as the moral police force of all human behaviour, it will trip itself up on its own righteousness just as we have.

One of the difficulties for Church at present when any issue of failure comes up is that she can only see it as contrary to the ideals of the Gospel and as an exposure of the hypocrisy of some of her members. This is no more than was promised by the Gospel – what was done in secret would be made known and what was hidden would be told from the rooftops. But the Church would rather it went away and might even try to push it under the carpet. This approach feeds the notion that she must be unblemished, immaculate all the time. It forgets that this is not so, but, more importantly, it forgets that there is a Gospel opportunity in every human situation – even the bad one. I believe when one of these arises we need to acknowledge it for what it is – sin in some form, failure to behave as Christians. Where people have been hurt our first concern must be for their interests, and only secondly for our own. If the hurt is in the public domain, by whatever means, then that acknowledgement, that concern and regret has to be expressed in the public domain too. To speak out of that frame of mind is to speak the word of the Gospel – a word of truth, a word of understanding, a word seeking forgiveness. For an individual, or the Church, to seek forgiveness and to offer what can be done by way of restoration, is to witness to redemption, and to the presence of the Pentecostal gift of the Spirit – 'whose sins you shall forgive they are forgiven'. This is not a sign of dissolution and death but rather a Gospel sign sorely needed in our harsh and unforgiving world. It is a privilege to have had the opportunity to speak it even if it were better that the situation which caused it had never happened.

Mutual prejudice

Perhaps *the* most serious dynamic at the heart of the Church/media dialogue is their capacity, or lack of it, to 'hear' each other. It often seems that the phrase 'you only hear what you want to hear' applies very much to Church/media interaction and conversations. It seems there is a real need to recognise the reality of prejudice operating here. The Church is prejudiced in so far as she is suspicious of media because the methods they sometimes use might be fast-track, overly simplistic, selective, intrusive or basically anti-Church, and in that context she will only hear coverage as negative or inadequate. Avoidance and evasion results. You could say that the Church is then refusing to pay her taxes to the media! 'Render unto Caesar....' To quote Cardinal Daly, speaking at the re-opening of Veritas last year, 'It is strange that we who talk so much about the need for dialogue and trust in the North, seem to be ourselves so wary of dialogue with media people and so lacking in trust of journalists.'

Media, on the other hand, seem suspicious of Church as never telling the truth, being overly protective, secretive and as this massive monolithic power controlling people's lives. If you speak out the truth as you know it there is a tendency in some media to assume that because you are Church it must be only half the truth. My experience is that there cannot be dialogue in this kind of atmosphere and the wedge of prejudice on both sides only gets wider. Communication and participation are a long way off and friendship is only a dream.

Prejudice not only deafens, it also blinds. I considered

using the biblical phrase 'the blind leading the blind' as a title for this presentation! One of my most difficult experiences was dealing with not being believed by some journalists, not just about substantive issues but about obvious verifiable practicalities, even when verification was available. In many cases and especially in the tabloid press, it seems that basic common sense and judgement go out the window when anything to do with Church is on the agenda. This is a feature of society in general today, and it poses a serious question for us as to how we have contributed to that perception. I would expect something more balanced, however, from those who seek to communicate the truth, the facts, the reality. But prejudice rears its head very easily!

Church belongs to society, and to the times that are in it, just as much as the media does, though at times one could be forgiven for thinking otherwise. Both are bound to reflect the evolution of the thought, perceptions and values of today because both are peopled by the contemporary struggles of humanity. Those like myself who belong to Church in a very public way and those who belong as active and committed members, do not live in a completely enclosed world and do not come from some alien planet. We are people of our own time, living in the same society as everybody else; we are not stupid or moronic or brainwashed and controlled, at least no more than anyone else is around us! We are not in the Church for power any more than others are in the media for power, or indeed anyone else is in any other field of endeavour. I believe that the great majority of people who function in the various dimensions of society are basically decent and good-living people. Naturally, like other areas, we will have our share of mavericks. That is to be expected, but of course it is not expected, and that is part of our problem. All major organisations and groupings suffer being tarred because of the failures of some members. Witness the recent coverage about refugees in this country. The Church suffers this blanket rejection perhaps more than most. No Church person may fail without the whole Church being the subject of ridicule, and yet a renegade garda, teacher, nurse, doctor, journalist or politician does not seem to bring opprobrium on their respective professions to the same degree. Why is that? Such prejudice is certainly calculated to clog up the channels of communication.

Today, it often seems as if Church is presented as the archaic, out-of-date, lost-cause body, while the media are the modern, ultra-bright, young institution. Whatever the truth of the leanings, such absolute characterisation is unhelpful. Conversation between two polarities can never be anything but an on-guard, raw prejudice. There is a parallel in the difficult interaction between the two traditions in the North. It seems to me that in this day and age such a way of operating is unworthy of two significant, competent, free and responsible institutions. Could I make a plea here for each body to begin to take the other more seriously as valuable, valid and positive dimensions of society? Could each institution pay the other the basic compliment of mutual respect, of accepting the other's word as 'yes' meaning yes and 'nay' meaning nay? This is not to negate in any way due and proper critique by either side. And there will be failures of course – but they can be dealt with appropriately without putting the whole dialogue at risk.

Perhaps we can all say that the Church has brought the trouble on herself over the years with her emphasis on secrecy and her enormous power. I accept that criticism; but we must move on from here, and today many Church organisations and spokespersons are genuine in their efforts to change that pattern to one of openness, truth and compassion. The change can be thwarted, however, by meeting a dogged prejudice which says something like 'don't try to change your ways, we always want you to be a big ogre whom we can continue to attack'! There are times when that attitude is only thinly disguised in the comments of quite reputable journalists.

Of course you could say that the Church is already in the media and the media in the Church in so far as nowadays many clerical and religious people have acquired the skills of journalism, and of radio/television presentation and production. Some clerical journalists commented on our situation last year in a serious and responsible way, seeking information and interviews as one would expect. Others commented, but out of the prevailing fashion of roundly castigating us. None of them contacted me as spokesperson at the time. Their inadequate research and strange desire to get on the Church-bashing bandwagon surprised me. I didn't see that at work where clerical abuse was at stake. Was it because we were women? Was it a safe situation on which to be on the winning side, so to speak, singing from the same hymn-sheet as some of their journalistic peers? If members of the Church are to work in the media world it seems to me it must be with a somewhat different focus than that of the secular press. There is a special onus on them to go after the truth and not to jump on the prevailing bandwagon. Is not our agenda that of communion rather than of persecution?

Despite that experience I would strongly call for an end to the culture of silence in the Church – silence when we are on the mat and when an explanation at least is required; or another silence which decides to say nothing because it is assumed that common sense will prevail and the vocals are only a small minority! Legal reasons are sometimes presented as the reasons for silence. We must live within the law of the land of course; but we need to guard lest legalities smother the Gospel as they did with the ancient Israelites. Given the influence of the media today, it is critical that we speak because it cannot be assumed that in all cases common sense, truth or compassion will prevail. In this context it is necessary to acquire the skills of media work so as to be able and confident, and even anxious, to speak for the sake of the Gospel. Many of the former situations in which Church had a ready listening audience have dried up. Must she not take the situations which present themselves now to proclaim the word of God, however difficult? We need not be afraid, for we have the promise of Christ: 'The spirit of God will speak through you' (Mt 10:20). Communication is at the service of society, and the responsibility of every institution is to contribute to the cohesion, participation and inclusion of all, whatever their hue. Communication is ultimately for communion.

Societal anger

A key issue for Church and media is to understand and read correctly the society in which they both live and which both seek to serve in different ways. It seems to me that there is a great subterranean anger in our present-day society which can be related to childhood. I am not a sociologist or a psychologist but I sense it has to do with a deep rejection of dominance, authority and ownership of person. I say subterranean because it is not immediately accessible but is reflected in the unprecedented generation gap, in the inability to understand the Ireland of the 1940s-60s, in the individualism that replaces the strong communal neighbourhood of the past, in the reaction of today's adults to the 'control' exercised by their own parents or authority figures in the past. This seems to be a world-wide phenomenon, as it is emerging in Canada, in Australia and New Zealand. But for us I wonder if it doesn't have something to do with our historical experience, and rejection, of the dominance of Britain over the centuries. In this century that was removed, but perhaps it was replaced very quickly by new 'dominations' – Church being the most powerful and effective, but also state and schools and disciplinarian parents. And I wonder if media is not being added to that list today.

This anger seems to take on the dimensions of hysteria at times – witness the reaction to all priests whenever there is a reported sex scandal, or the recent hysteria over refugees. In spite of our apparent sophistication at the end of the twentieth century we have not come to terms with our own recent and speedy evolution. We look around for someone to blame every time there is a crisis or a failure. We are a fragile and in many ways phobia-oriented people. How much of this anger is recognised by the Church or media? Do they seek to understand it? Or do they wittingly or unwittingly feed it? Is the state aware of this anger which seems to have to do with childhood ... often one's own childhood? I believe this anger was very evident last year and that it reached the level of hysteria at times. It is not for me to question the grounds for that, but I do raise the question about the appropriateness of some reporting which seemed to whip up the hysteria rather than bring a calm, balanced and well-researched contribution to the issue. Only media can redress its own excesses and it is encouraging to see that happening both in the print and TV outlets, and sometimes at considerable cost to those journalists involved.

Childhood is related to family and family is an ideal, an

unrealised ideal in many ways, but some form of it remains the aspiration of all for a wholesome and integrated life. It has of course failed its young people in many instances. Sadly in some cases parents separate, or cannot provide adequate care, or fall down in their responsibilities. Children are the losers and anything less than family will never be other than a poor substitute. Such a life situation, however practically good, has inherent and unavoidable pain and perhaps anger. But it is a myth to think that life within the family was or is a guaranteed garden of Eden. Many who had lost family seemed to think it was like that in every case. Overly strict discipline, poor communication and inadequate parenting within the family were more common than we care to admit and often brought unhappiness that left scars for many years. The pressures of family violence and break-up may be different today but they bring hardship and pain nonetheless.

As Church and media we would do well to listen to the voice of those who were denied family in the past, because the children who are deprived of a parent today, for whatever reason, will make their pain and anger known as they reach adulthood. Children who are the almost careless result of adult activity, or who are a required possession for adult fulfilment, will live to speak their searing questions: 'Why did you have me? Why did you leave me? Why did you ignore my needs and rights?' All of us – Church, media and society – will look back at our politically correct approaches to young people today and know that we failed them.

Competitive drive

Media are very much in the market economy. Selling papers is the goal. Standards and accuracy can easily come second to sales. Sensationalism, based on the strange and crude or the immediate, helps to whet the consumerist appetite. A short time ago I heard a serious radio discussion on the amount of programmes and articles dealing with the issue of exams in recent years. This year there seems to be a better balance, and of course some sections always attempted to be reasonable. Because it is topical and seasonal, because it is close to the vulnerable and worried student, the media went into this area in a big way, playing on the stress and supplying all sorts of 'helps' which are all available in the pupil's school context in a calm and comprehensive way. One psychologist at this discussion described what the media were doing as exam pornography. Strong language but very real and close to the bone. Competition and consumerism bring this about and it has little to do with community or the general good of already stressed young students.

I recognise and very much respect a number of fine journalists working in the electronic and print media outlets and have every reason to be grateful to some of them for their generous persistence and professionalism in seeking out the truth behind the scenes. However, it would seem that their editors and producers often have a wider range of values, because the same outlets will give space to others who would seem to do less than careful work. Investigative journalism is a real service to society and I believe fully in it. But it has taken a battering for me after last year. I have less confidence in its accuracy. I was shocked by the poor research and the inadequate efforts at verification which I saw in operation. That might be countered by 'why not sue if the media has got it wrong?' Why should we? Journalists are well-educated people and ought to be able to provide well-researched copy. Besides, we as Church are not much inclined to sue; and because that is known it seems that liberties are sometimes taken with accuracy and objectivity. I think it was C. P. Scott who said 'comment is free; facts are sacred'. The media have a real obligation to set and monitor standards among their own members if they wish for co-operation from others or if they wish to bring other groups, including Church, to task. It seems to me that the selling-of-papers goal at times allows for shabby, shallow and sometimes seriously misleading coverage. Imaginative composition is another result of the market-driven media. If the body in question will not come forward, or the story is without sufficient spark (as in the recent election), reporting and reality may be poles apart. This only serves to widen wedges of division and cynicism. A reticent Church contributes to misleading coverage and must take its share of the blame. Each of us must earn respect in the societal milieu – it is not something to be demanded. Because of our task, neither of us can afford to pinch on that.

The electronic media, particularly TV, speak to the emotional, affective and symbolic dimensions of our life. This is a great leap forward in the whole field of communication because in the past the printed word spoke mainly to the reason and intellect, leaving a large undeveloped lacuna in the person's capacity to know and understand the world and experience. Television knows full well the power of the picture, that wordless communication that speaks volumes and makes for good TV. But it is possible to abuse that power, to play the prejudice card or the market-forces card with people's non-verbal feelings and fears. To repeat an evocative picture which subconsciously entrenches a negative symbol will consequently close the avenues of communication, if not worse, for many years ahead rather than bring about collaboration and reconciliation.

Adversarial approach

Another dynamic which affects the dialogue between our two institutions is the adversarial approach in common usage. We know that this approach is how our justice and court system works and we have problems with it. It is often harsh, destructive and inhuman in its search for justice. It is certainly not very feminine and is often very patriarchal. It operates something like this: say the worst about your opponent and hear the worst back about yourself. It then hopes to weigh the balance between the two worsts and name the least worst as the winner! It seems that our political world operates on much the same premise, if the recent election and other events are anything to go by. In the media I wonder if the tactic is to flush out your opponent by provocation. That might be a good hunting or fishing tactic and very macho, but it is also downright uncivilised. It seems to me to smack of the Dark Ages and has little to do with an adult, responsible search for the truth.

This approach seems to be very evident in radio and TV chat shows and interviews. Pursuing this adversarial approach between Church and media gives the sense of being in a war situation, where each is looking for a way to undermine the other. Communication is not at work. Rather, some kind of megaphone war is taking place, and war is destructive whatever the weapons used. The so-called Cold War was a war of words, silence and mutual loathing between the parties. Neither communication nor communion is achieved by the adversarial approach and it is hard to see how it contributes to the good of society.

The court system may argue that the adversarial method has much to recommend it. But there at least, it is managed by qualified and skilled professionals who are properly appointed to the task of searching for justice and fairness. On the other hand, the media, in many cases, seem to take the position of self-appointed prosecutor, judge and jury. They seem to want to bypass the appropriate structures for accountability in the state. This approach is not calculated to inspire confidence, and still less so when accompanied by cynically inadequate or biased research.

Feminine deficit?

Is there anything which can be seen as feminine about Church/media relations? The Church is easily identified with the lack of the feminine and with a predominance of the male; she is considered the last bastion of male preserve! Her personnel and methods are deeply embedded in the hierarchical mode. Openness, risk, participation and inclusion do not come easy to her. However, it has been said loudly enough to her; she acknowledges her failure, if somewhat reluctantly and less than wholeheartedly. One could say she is making some efforts to redress the balance.

Are the media doing the same? Are they open to criticism in this area? I don't see very much of the feminine in the media approach to issues, people or problems. Neither is it very obvious in its structures, personnel or pursuit of consumerism. Glaring headlines, aggression, bullying and the dynamics of verbal blood sport seem to be acceptable. I don't find anything very feminine there – in fact, many headlines and approaches are so problematic that they cancel out the valuable reporting. Professor George Gerbner, an internationally known media expert, says that 'in the world of news men outnumber women six to one ... the media world is skewed not in the direction of life but in the direction of power ... it is a world packaged for sale and power' (Manila,

1989). You cannot expect credibility when your own tools reflect the wrongdoing you are criticising in the first place. To lift a hammer over the people you considered wielded a hammer over you, or over others, hardly shows that we are making any progress as a civilisation.

As a woman in and of the Church and a woman of my time, affected deeply by an increasing consciousness of the absence of the reflective, the intuitive, nurturing dimensions from our institutional life for so long, I view this dialogue as one critically requiring a balanced perspective which includes the feminine. The core values of a feminine consciousness are equality, openness, interconnectedness, compassion, listening, plurality. The pursuit of truth, forgiveness, healing and reconciliation are not helped by the hyping of prejudice, anger and consumerist values. A more feminine Church and a more feminine media would lead to a more wholesome and caring society.

Conclusion

How then can we both work so that our dialogue leads to communion? Genuine communication is as essential to the quality of life as food, shelter and health care. It is part of every aspect of life and therefore is the responsibility of everyone. The Church, as a socially responsible institution in society, must be and must become a better organ of communication. And that communication must be open, transparent and truthful. It must come into play when the Church is in trouble, when she is accused of failure, just as much as when other matters of importance to her perspective are at issue. Above all, that communication needs to be compassionate; if that is not a priority for the media (and I would ask why not?) it surely must be a priority for the Church; our communication needs to be a witness to the capacity of the human being by the grace of God to act lovingly whatever the situation. Such communication leads to communion.

Negative communication from either the Church or the media creates an environment of destruction. For the good of our society the question is not 'can we be friends?' but 'can we afford not to be friends?' The Church has held the high ground for centuries. She spoke without fear of contradiction from the pulpit. Her sway in that piece of furniture has been severely curbed. But the media are now moving in that direction, nearing the pulpit! There is a great responsibility on them to handle it better than we did!

REPORTING CHURCH NEWS

Joe Little

I have been asked to speak about my experience of meeting the demands of public service broadcasting and dealing with the Churches on matters of concern to the general public.

A little over a generation ago the question would not have been put in that way. Up until the early 1960s, journalists – in the Republic certainly – generally met the demands, not so much of the public, but of the Roman Catholic Church, which effectively determined what was of public concern on a wide range of matters, and what was to be done about them.

Before he retired as primate, I recall Cardinal Cahal Daly reflecting on this era of the Church ascendant. He apologised to writers and artists in particular for their suffering under Church-inspired censorship. In my view, the Cardinal's apology creates space for reconciliation between media and Church. There is a need for writers working in the secularised media – and Catholics who want to hand on important values – to understand each other's focusing on the present and obsession by the past. I am conscious that by setting ourselves up as a moral police force, we journalists could easily trip up on our own righteousness. But a rapidly changing society needs ethical reference points. Violence and avarice are frequently accepted and glamorised both inside and outside the media. And since the Watergate revelations, in particular, many journalists feel a vocation to expose wrongdoing, even when they do not see occasional flaws in their own behaviour.

But can either journalists or Church members seek to construct some kind of ethical safety-net to promote the common good without offending the common moral sense of individuals, and this without becoming arrogant and hypocritical? I don't know, but I think the problem is worth addressing.

Since taking up my present post at the end of 1994, I have reported more than my share of apologies. On behalf of the Church of Ireland, the Primate, Dr Eames, said sorry for the conversions of poor Catholics by the Anglican Soupers during the Great Famine.

A small group of Presbyterians apologised for the violence surrounding last year's march from Drumcree. And Bishop Willie Walsh's apology for the hurt caused by Rome's *ne temere* decree is still causing ripples – positive and negative – months later. Where Church and media are concerned, Bishop Thomas Flynn called for the return of that good old virtue of forgiveness. From the media side, which is far from prefect, I echo his plea.

Clerical sex abuse

During my thirty or so months as RTÉ's religious and social affairs correspondent, sexual abuse – proven and alleged – by Catholic clergy and religious, of young people entrusted to their care, has been the single most controversial issue I have dealt with. A psychologist for the Granada Centre in Dublin has spoken of over fifty priests and religious coming into care for counselling in this area. In October 1995, the bishops claimed that about one and a half per cent of their diocesan clergy – or about fifty-seven priests – have had allegations made against them or have been convicted. The figures for religious orders were not available. In March 1996, the then Catholic Primate Cardinal Daly said:

> The media have discharged their rightful function in reporting these scandals. The space given ... can well be said to be disproportionate; but this reflects the place held by Catholic clergy in public esteem and trust in Ireland, and the particular horror evoked by the abuse of that esteem and that trust. I believe the media have done a service to the Church in this regard.
>
> The truth can be painful, but it is also healing and liberating ... humbled and penitent bishops and priests can be better bearers of Christ's message of repentance, humility and service.

But Dr Daly went on to say that allegations of scandal had been reported 'sometimes with scant regard for the pain and the rights of the subjects of these allegations'.

On balance, I think history will record that RTÉ News' treatment of these cases was truthful and served the public interest. We are talking about the period after Fr Brendan Smyth's wrongdoing was disclosed in court in the North, a period when the Church authorities admitted they had, over a long period, great difficulty curbing the offender or understanding the nature of the offence, and, therefore, a period when, for the first time in Ireland, survivors of abuse needed encouragement to come forward if they had genuine complaints to make.

At that time, there were no guidelines for the Catholic Church in Ireland, but guidelines for dealing with sexual abuse issued by the Catholic Church in England and Wales also took the view that parishes must be told if a priest, religious or Church employee is under investigation because, according to their guiding principle, 'the interest of the child [was] paramount'. But I wonder if the Irish bishops, who have adopted the same principle, have taken any legal advice on whether the rights of subjects of allegations can properly be relegated to second place behind the interests of the child? Do the other denominations here have a view?

General sexual abuse

I combine the roles of religious and social affairs correspondent. In covering social affairs, I have also had the opportunity to report on sexual abuse in the wider society – where fathers abuse children, or where disabled people are victims of sexual assault, for example. I have no doubt from these experiences that victims and the wider society need more support and resources to come to terms with perpetrators who in many cases may not be reformable. Winston Churchill said that a society is judged by how it treats its weakest members. It seems to me that our challenge now is how to treat both survivors and perpetrators of sexual abuse. In the United States, the Catholic diocese of Minnesota was instrumental in setting up the Hazelden Centre, which invented the Twelve Steps programme of Alcoholics Anonymous. At the time, it was coming to terms with the heavy drinking of some priests. Out of despair came hope. I have no doubt that many Church people here can face the lessons of the past three years in Ireland and bring forward some good from them.

Media

Earlier in the Conference we heard from my executive editor in RTÉ News, Dermot Mullane, about the formal laws, rules and guidelines which determined standards in our newsroom. I think it may be useful to add some words on the informal demands made on us by the rapidly changing news industry. Among these are the expectations:

1. To be first with the news, as it breaks
During each day, this requires us to simultaneously service radio bulletins, the *Morning Ireland* programme and *The News at One,* together with a vastly expanded number of television bulletins, which are now broadcast on the hour.

2. To tell the story in less than two minutes

3. Not to be repetitive – to find new material for our stories as the day progresses
If an editor of an evening bulletin sees my story on the *One O'Clock* TV News, he/she may be reluctant to re-broadcast the same material on the *Six-One.* So it often needs updating, with reaction.

Radio sub-editors are correctly reluctant to carry repeats of reports carried on bulletins two or three hours earlier. RTÉ is, after all, competing with a vibrant independent radio sector, with both local and national news services. Customers will twirl the button if they feel news is unreasonably repetitive.

4. To interview the main actors in the day's/week's developments
Interviewees are the life-blood of radio and television news, from *Morning Ireland* at its earlier time of 7.30 a.m. to *Network News* at 10.30 p.m. on the second television channel, to *This Week* on Sundays.

5. *To use the new technologies*

Thanks to satellite and microwave communications, RTÉ has revolutionised news-gathering in very recent times. Both radio and television can now use two satellite vans to beam back live interviews or to edit and send reports from any location nationwide and from many places abroad. A terrestrial link van can do the same in the Greater Dublin area. Effectively, this means that if a story is considered sufficiently important, it can be covered instantly on location. Until two years ago all interviewees and videotape had to be brought to an RTÉ studio in the regions or to Montrose.

These developments create more and more pressure on the journalist's scarcest resource, which is not good will, but time. And for that reason, I beg your understanding when I approach you urgently about topics which you believe deserve greater reflection. But I also invite you to use the growing opportunities RTÉ News can offer you if you want to say your piece.

USING THE MESSAGE
USING THE SYMBOLS

Dermod McCarthy

Background

We are, as a leading philosopher in the University of Edinburgh observed recently, living in an increasingly coercive society, but a society which coerces us to be tentative about the rightness or wrongness of society, where parents are expected to say to their children 'Whatever you think is right for you, darling, that's what you should do!' As a result we are experiencing a fragmentation of society and a fragmentation of the self.

It was interesting to hear the words of introduction by the former secretary general of the United Nations, Mr Boutros Boutros-Ghali when the Pope addressed the General Assembly of the United Nations on its fiftieth anniversary two years ago. I could expect a spiritual leader to express these thoughts but it was quite significant that the chief executive of the world's largest secular organisation spoke as follows when he introduced Pope John Paul to the Assembly:

> Belief in a higher reality provides a common bond among nations but the horrors we witness today deny the values of the Spirit. Terrible examples on every continent tell us that to deny our spiritual nature is to diminish our God. A crisis of the human spirit is taking

place. It accounts for many of the major problems of our time. We must make it possible for people to regain their faith.

There is a person, in a position of world leadership, who obviously recognises that human society today needs to be reminded about God's presence in our world.

Given the depth of penetration which television enjoys in every home and individual in western society today, there is no doubt that television programmes dealing with such discussion of our human and spiritual destiny are an essential part of the broadcasting schedule. We are not looking for a special reverence for religious programmes, nor do we seek a special place for the Christian, Jewish or Orthodox view of the world. We simply ask that religion and the spiritual dimension be acknowledged as a constituent part of human life and that it be recognised as such by those who allocate resources within broadcasting organisations. In other words, that religion be treated with the same seriousness and respect as politics, current affairs, education, art, agriculture, environment issues and so on.

Of course, because our society is increasingly a market-place of competing interests, one of which is the Church, broadcasters are faced with a dilemma. What can we take for granted? What are the expectations of viewers in relation to religion on television, or listeners to religion on radio? What do they want? There is no longer a uniform opinion, a common view.

Another difficulty comes from those who believe that the message of the Gospel is too important, too sacred, too awesome, or even too difficult to be left to the trivialising tendencies of broadcasting. They would say that while it might be genuine religion that enters the broadcasting system at one end, what emerges at the other is entertainment.

Both my Church of Ireland colleague and I receive letters from time to time criticising minute departures from strict liturgical norms in Sunday morning television Masses and Services. Sometimes these are necessitated by technical or pastoral reasons, but no excuse will satisfy the purists!

Then there are those pious people who interpret the public service broadcasting brief of RTÉ – the Irish national broadcasting organisation – in such a way that they want it to help them return Irish society to a golden age when everybody went to church and the family Rosary was said on bended knee in the kitchen.

I regularly get letters asking me to arrange for the broadcast of the joyful mysteries of the Rosary after the 6 p.m. News each day – because, as one woman wrote, 'It is no longer being said in Irish homes'.

In the film version of *The Field,* you may remember, in the final powerful scene, the Bull McCabe strides to the sea in frustration and anger, beating back the tide with his stick. Some people still believe that religious television can perform similar feats.

What kind of religion should we broadcast and how do we resolve the tensions that sometimes arise between those who are ministers of religion, and professional programme makers who must try to ensure that the maximum number of viewers will watch their programmes – religious or otherwise?

Different languages

The Churches and media institutions, by and large, inhabit different spaces, are mutually suspicious of each other and have contrasting perceptions of the world around them. They speak different languages. It is very important for each to try, at least, to understand not only the language, but the imperatives that drive each other.

In our increasingly secular society, broadcasting a sense of who God is and what God's message is about, requires people who can develop a new language, a language which continues to speak to people's deepest longings and hopes but which rekindles a sense of meaning and purpose in life, a language which can speak on the one hand to the committed while making intellectual and spiritual sense to the uncommitted. But it is also a language that has to be expressed in the most powerful, arresting and challenging images and symbols possible, because that is the kind of world we are in.

Church and media

The Catholic Church has always had an ambivalent attitude to the media. No sooner was the book invented than the Church fought against its influence by introducing the index. Its attitude to the electronic media was equally negative at the beginning. Even still, there is a serious under-estimation of the need for media training and for an appreciation of the powerful contribution which broadcasters can make either to promote or to hinder the message of the Gospel.

In May two years ago, the Irish Government issued a Green Paper on the future of broadcasting in Ireland. It invited comments from all interested parties before September of that year. After the summer meeting of the Irish Catholic hierarchy, I asked one of the bishops if they had decided to send in a submission. To my amazement he told me it had never been mentioned and asked 'Should we have?' I pointed out that when a Green Paper on Education was issued a few years ago, they had held meetings, consulted experts and submitted a long document to the Department of Education, yet they had nothing to say and no guidance to give about something which will exert at least as much if not more influence on the minds of future generations of Irish people.

The absence of such official involvement leaves the field clear for fundamentalists of all kinds. We are familiar with the phenomenon of the tele-evangelists, and we are suspicious of their middle-class, cosy, non-challenging brand of Christianity, backed up by big money and big business. It also makes it possible for ultra-conservative Catholics to develop and expand religious channels on cable systems in the US and Europe, broadcasting a constant diet of anti-ecumenical, nostalgic, pre-Vatican II Catholicism.

People involved in making religious broadcasts are trying to explore what faith is doing in the world, and sharing the ambiguities, the certainties and the doubts about values and beliefs. It happens in our worship programmes, in our documentaries and magazine programmes, and in short programmes of meditation and reflection as we struggle to interpret the pain and suffering of our society in the light of eternity. It is not our job to preach – that is the task of the parish clergy, but it is our role to be pre-evangelists, examining changing attitudes, banishing ignorance and prejudice, allowing people to tell their stories, sowing seeds, floating ideas.

As Stephen Whittle, former head of Religious Broadcasting at the BBC, once said, 'We are involved in the intriguing business of keeping the rumour of God alive at the heart of the machine'.

The broadcasting context

Just as the context within which we live affects our approach to matters of faith and morals, so too it affects the whole broadcasting industry. Broadcasting is undergoing rapid and radical change – not all of it for the better.

When parliamentarians were drawing up legislation for commercial TV channels throughout Europe in the 1980s, they failed to pay sufficient attention to what was going to be on these channels. Neither did they listen to those who were expressing grave concern. Now that they have let the genie out of the bottle, with a free-for-all and open trans-frontier availability of programming, they realise too late that we are now reaping a whirlwind. Consequently, the attitude of the public will and must carry more and more weight in deciding what television programmes are offered and what will be regarded as likely to gain an audience.

One of my Belgian colleagues, Ernest Henau, pointed out in a recent article that when we come to religious matters being covered in television programmes, there are immediate and special problems. For a start, there is a perceived incompatibility between a thoughtful approach on commercial and public service channels, which gets in the way of in-depth treatment of any serious subjects. Prime time television is a difficult place for nuanced treatment of any spiritual matters. Also, television is about symbols, and the media prefer to use symbolic figures as spokespersons. A cardinal, an archbishop, or a charismatic and media-friendly prelate will be asked to appear again and again. They are considered to speak more in the name of all their flock than, for example, are lay people.

And yet, the journalists who ask those people to appear are the same journalists who will criticise the Church for not giving more prominence to lay opinion.

Another difficulty arises from our emphasis on the unusual, the sensational, the alternative, whatever is contrary to the general norm. If broadcasters give space to those who they think hold power, they also give preference to those who challenge this real or imaginary power. And so, some controversial minority groups or people take on a significance or weight that they do not in fact have. As a result, broadcasters often confer legitimacy on people or groups simply because they perform well on television rather than because of the substance of their arguments or the size of their following.

There is also the difficulty which arises from television reporters presenting news and views about religious matters, when they themselves are totally uninterested in religion, and do not believe in God. It is almost impossible for them to be familiar with the way in which believers see their faith and to share in the mystery which is at the heart of all belief. So the only way they can interpret the standpoint of the Church on an issue of faith or morality is by imposing a political grid on the subject, and viewing it in terms of a government and its opposition, right or left opinions. The fact that by its nature the Church organisation is at the service of the world, as Vatican II stressed again and again, is never or very rarely presented.

The result is that by explaining the religious institution through political categories, people come to regard it in reality much more in terms of power than in terms of service.

Need for media education
One of our problems in Ireland is the scarcity of articulate and balanced lay Catholic intellectuals. Since Vatican II more and more people are aware of their responsibility in the Church

but they are shy of coming forward to participate in religious programmes on radio or television as thinkers and leaders of opinion. One of our prominent newspaper columnists, John Waters of *The Irish Times,* wrote a feature article on this point last year, entitled 'Filling the God-Shaped Hole'.

The Church has its own responsibilities in relation to broadcasting and to media in general. Education in the use of media and in the Christian reception of media is essential for lay people, religious and priests. It is particularly needed by parents, educators and children. The document *Aetatis novae* and a whole series of papal documents of the past quarter century stress the need for all Christians to be properly formed and equipped for living in a media society. *Aetatis novae* states:

> Today's evangelisation ought to well up from the Church's active sympathetic presence within the world of communications.

Pope Paul VI and Pope John Paul II stressed that the use of media in catechesis and in evangelisation is essential. *Aetatis novae* states:

> Education and training in communications should be an integral part of the formation of pastoral workers and priests.

The Church must try to be accessible to media. It must have lines of communication open to media, not in order unduly or improperly to try to influence them, but rather 'in the spirit of honest and respectful dialogue', and in order to offer help and co-operation which might assist media in their role of 'contributing to the human right of true information'.

The Church has no reason to be afraid of media. Rather, if it believes that it has a vitally important message to communicate to the world, it should be doing so unashamedly with the same degree of polish and professionalism which leading broadcasting organisations apply to programmes in sport and entertainment.

Sadly, this is not yet happening. In an increasingly competitive world, in which production standards in broadcasting are improving in leaps and bounds, there is still too much complacency and amateurism in the attitude of the Catholic Church to the broadcasting of its message. I have seen this at every level in the organisation – from the dull coverage of papal events in the Vatican, to the over-defensive and hesitant release of information after meetings of national hierarchies, the unwillingness on the part of too many priests to prepare in a professional manner for broadcast Masses, and the great reluctance of both clergy and informed lay people to champion and proclaim their beliefs on a whole variety of television and radio programmes.

Only by seeking the best possible methods of communication of the Christian message can Church people, lay and clerical, gain the respect that the Church should have in the marketplace.

Core questions

Dietrich Bonhoeffer was a modern prophet who, from his prison in Nazi Germany, asked the question which is at the centre of our theme – how to broadcast the reality of God to a secular society that feels no need of the concept, and is not even aware it is deprived? Who is God for us here and now?

How do we meet him and how do we help others to meet him today? These are enormous and vital questions for a communicator to ask.

Lord Soper said once that the Christian Churches were providing answers to questions that no one was asking any longer. Bonhoeffer pointed out that God has been pushed to that fringe area of life where human knowledge gives out or human despair begins – the 'God of the gaps', as he put it.

The modern marketplace

I suggest that it is in helping people to situate God *within* the suffering, the pain, the doubts, the anxieties of our times that we can best fulfil the role of Christian broadcasters in today's frantic world. But it means that the Church must be in the marketplace, with its own attractive stall, raising her voice and proclaiming her wares, as professionally and as competently as all the other stall-holders.

St Paul did not hesitate to do so in his time, nor must we in ours.

Our task as Christian broadcasters is to remind people of God and to present the message of the Gospel in new apparel. It is the task of the Church to enable people to actually come into God's presence.

THE CHURCH AND THE MEDIA CAN THEY BE FRIENDS?

Pat Heneghan

I confine my remarks largely to the subject of the Roman Catholic Church merely because I can most usefully speak about what I know best.

There's a special theme for this section: 'The Church and Media – Servants, or Friends?' Well, I found this a bit puzzling. Did anyone in Ireland ever think of the press as a servant of the Church? But then I thought back to a period not so long ago. During the 1950s and early 1960s, the idea that the media should serve the Church might not have been stated or expressed, but it was widely held. Service, if not servitude, and friendship, was precisely what the media in this country offered the Catholic Church.

The Church could rely on media to put out a line that was, broadly speaking, not merely favourable to her individual actions, deeds and policies, but was supportive of her underlying interests and beliefs.

It is, I think you will agree with me, very hard, in 1997, to remember with absolute clarity, even for those of us old enough to have been around at the time, how things were then. It was indeed extraordinary, the extent to which the Church could rely on layers upon layers of protection from probing eyes, and also from the cut and thrust of open debate on doctrine or morality.

It is partly, of course, that during a period like the 1940s and 1950s, great institutions like the Church, the Government, large companies, and so on, enjoyed the kind of general respect that was an element of the more authoritarian climate of the time. But it was more than that. The Church, I think, enjoyed a special immunity. The frailties and failings which we now know to have existed in the Church were simply not acknowledged at all.

From *The Irish Press* and *The Irish Independent,* from Radio Éireann, and even from Telefís Éireann in the early days, the Church could be assured of respectful treatment. Even *The Irish Times* kept out of things, happy to cater to its traditional readership, most of whom considered themselves not dependent on the good graces of Mother Church, nor on her Church-run schools or hospitals.

It is curious to note that, in *The Irish Independent,* this cordial relationship continued from the time of William Martin Murphy at the turn of the century, right up to the takeover by Tony O'Reilly in the early 1970s. It continued, perhaps with the odd hiccup, during Dr O'Reilly's ownership, only to be shattered by the events of the last few years. The writers of Middle Abbey Street have reported those events with as much bravery and thoroughness, not to say relish, as their colleagues in *The Irish Times* or *The Belfast Newsletter.*

Similarly, RTÉ and all its predecessors, in all its stations and manifestations, were duly deferential, reflecting, like the national newspapers, the respect and reverence in which the Church was held by the overwhelming majority of the Irish people.

The 1960s brought familiarity and informality – singing priests and nuns and media-wise bishops – but little diminution in power, which the hierarchy maintained throughout the 1970s and 1980s. If there was any ebbing away, it was slow, and almost unnoticed. It was almost as if the clergy themselves were in charge of the ebb, more than happy, as it were, to hand over some of their minor duties to an ever-faithful flock.

But then, towards the end of the 1980s, the damn burst and the power of the Church gushed away, while now, near the end of the 1990s, it has dried up, almost completely.

To be brutally candid: whatever support and respect that might remain is ageing and diminishing. It derives chiefly from those in my age bracket and above, who will take our old habits and loyalties with us to the grave, to be replaced quite possibly by no one, or perhaps just by a faithful few. And remember, this prognosis is coming from a friend.

Of course there are teenagers and young adults who are devout Catholics, but there is not at the moment even half enough of them to keep the Church from collapsing and dying, if not in my lifetime, at least in theirs. Unless, of course, something dramatic and unexpected happens, which it very well may.

When I say that support for the Church has crumbled away to nothing, I suppose I should try to explain and qualify.

Yes, of course you will, on occasion, see media coverage which, most often indirectly, reflects well on the Church. We will still read of priests, nuns and lay activists in the Church, working hard to bear witness to the Gospel of Jesus Christ, both by preaching that Gospel, and by living the Gospel in their daily work.

But now we come to my department: why do stories about such people seem to have no rehabilitative effect on the reputation of the Catholic Church as an institution?

Most such good works, most of the people doing them are likely to be seen and reported, if at all, in secular terms and in secular language: a column on the good work of Sister Stanislaus Kennedy, a photograph of a Catholic missionary feeding the hungry in Somalia, both of them dressed, probably in ordinary clothes; both of them seen, by the journalist if not by the reader, as political or humanitarian figures, and not chiefly as representatives of the Catholic Church.

I myself feel an overwhelming urge to moan and complain that none of the benign influence or guidance of the institutional Church is acknowledged or even mentioned in such stories. If the work of priests and nuns is shown at all, it is in this secularised context. But I will not moan. I will try instead to suggest why this might be happening.

But before we go any further, we should ask ourselves: Why bother trying to get a good press for the institution of the Catholic Church?

Lots of reasons: because it will help them continue to do good works, and help them in their support of those priests and lay members who do likewise; because every press report on the work of the Church bears in itself compelling witness to the value of the Christian message. There is one final reason for trying to get the Church a good press: because a good press will help the Church to hold on to her power.

Forgive me, again, for speaking bluntly. The Church is no more inclined than the Government or the banks or the trade unions to throw away her power, or to forfeit her ability to act as a power broker. Now, you cannot expect the public to be as sympathetic to this secondary goal, the wielding of power, as to the primary one, the preaching of the Gospel. These days, individual parishioners will respect and support their parish priest and his curates only in so far as they perceive that the respect and the power they grant them is a power for good, in the parish, in the diocese, in the wider community.

When those people feel that the Church has helped them develop, spiritually and intellectually and socially, they can act as powerful advocates. Now, how do you get these people on the air? You don't. Maybe you can try, but I don't think you should bother. Don't bother trying to have them packaged up by the Catholic Press and Information Office. Don't bother inviting editors and producers to look at the wonderful work done in the local youth club, or in the parish hall, or by the Medical Missionaries, or by the Sisters of Charity. You'd be wasting your time. I won't trouble you in this little talk with an analysis of the value of news, as perceived by editors and producers. But for our purposes it is enough to observe what the media covers, and what it doesn't.

Broadly speaking, good news is no news. You're wasting your time asking them to take an interest in what Wordsworth called

> ...that best portion of a good man's life,
> His little, nameless unremembered acts
> Of kindness and of love...

When a priest, as one of my acquaintance did recently, gives shelter to a pregnant unmarried mother, pays for her medical care, and fixes her up with a job, it's good news, but it's not necessarily dramatic. It is not even public. I found out about it not from the priest, but from the girl herself, who gave me permission to use her story as an example. It's a nice story, but it's not a train wreck. It's not a political scandal. It's not a drug deal. It's good news. And good news is no news.

I'm not blaming the editors. If anything, it's our fault. It's human nature. It's you and me, slowing down to gawp at a car accident.

Good news is no news. So there is little point in trying to stage-manage, and to package, the testimony of those lay people who feel that the Church is doing good. So let's not try to round up the usual suspects and get them on the air. Let us, rather, appeal to the usual suspects themselves.

As a layman I feel I can make an appeal in a way that a bishop might find unseemly. I can say to all of you who are still active in the Church: tell your own story. Bear your own witness. It doesn't have to be a religious story. It doesn't even have to be a 'feel-good' story in any kind of obvious way. The clergy do not need to have a starring role. But if the Church was there when you needed her, why not spread the good news?

The message that I would convey to this conference, and through this conference to the members of the Catholic Church, is this: if there are people – and I sense their presence on every *Pat Kenny Show,* on every *Late Late Show* on which the Church is being attacked – if there are people sitting there, seething and grinding their teeth, enduring yet another liberal Dublin 4 diatribe against their beloved Catholic Church, let them stop seething and start talking.

Talk quietly and without rancour. Don't attack the attackers. Instead, find a way to tell your story. If you can't tell that story on a talk show, or in a national newspaper, tell it at least to your children, or to your friends.

Because that story, ladies and gentlemen, and all those other stories, makes up the hidden reality. Quiet, relentless, thankless daily heroism: that is the reality of the Church at work in Ireland today.

You may not think of me as much of an expert on reality. Fair enough: after all, we in the priesthood of public relations do like to put our best foot forward, and to help our clients do likewise. But I am not speaking out of school when I say that when the bad news broke, as it did about the Bishop of Galway, and the paedophile scandals, and the problems of Goldenbridge, my advice to the hierarchy would have been to face reality. Own up. Take the blame. Accept the consequences. Tell the public you're sorry. Promise to do what you can to prevent a recurrence, and then keep those promises.

I am a supporter of the Church, and a believer in Christian ideals. But even those who are not, were aware that during the worst, the height of the clerical scandals, there were during that very period thousands of acts of heroism undertaken daily by the Church, and in its name by its members, lay and clerical.

The Church has attracted, and will I hope continue to attract, heroic people, quiet heroes many of them. They wish to dedicate their lives not merely to preaching the Gospel, but to recreating the Gospel message in the way they live.

Please understand one thing: when I suggest that the Church could benefit from third-party endorsement, I'm not looking for the job of rounding it up. In fact, I would specifically disqualify myself from that task. If public relations has a role at all it is a minor and supportive one. Perhaps the most useful thing I can do, is simply to goad the rest of you into speech and action and then let you get on with it.

As this young state crawls its way through infancy, and enters, as it has recently, a kind of national adolescence, we all seem to be blowing off steam. We all seem to be rebelling against the institutions and authority figures that exerted so much control over the childhood years of our young nation's history.

Politicians have been the target of a good deal of this rag, and so has the Church. Perhaps it's all part of the rites of passage, part of our painful maturing as a nation. Perhaps it's not altogether a bad thing.

So don't attack the attackers. Just remind them that, while some representatives of the Church have done some dreadful things, many more have achieved extraordinary amounts of good. Hard-working priests and nuns have built schools and hospitals, have created institutions from which they, the attackers, have probably benefited.

Let us not try to neutralise the negative messages we've all heard about the Church, because we needed to hear those messages. Let us try, rather, to think, and to talk, and to write about the great work that the Church continues to do.

That is my suggestion, and I think the lay people of this country can carry out that suggestion without my help, and without the direct involvement of the hierarchy.

As for the Church and the media being friends? Even if my suggestions are followed, I don't think that the Church and the media will ever again be 'friends' in the way that they used to be – and I think that is a good thing. Some of the best work the Church is doing in the modern world is being done under siege. It is being done in countries in which the Church has no friends in court: none in court or in parliament, and few enough in the press and the media.

Sometimes our priests and bishops fail us. If they get a bad press as a result, that is good, not bad. It means that bad behaviour is exposed, and that some kind of cleansing has a chance to take place.

Even when the Church is getting a bad press for its good deeds, that isn't the end of the world, either. The Church will always have to take unpopular positions, urging us to moderate our appetites, and to curb our impulses when the more primitive side of our nature prompts us, as Oscar Wilde put it, to resist everything, except temptation.

There is that joke in the Tom Stoppard play *Night and Day,* where the corrupt dictator tells the visiting journalist, 'I believe in a relatively free press. That is, a free press controlled by my relatives.' The Church may also get a bad press when it reminds such a dictator of his fallibility and his mortality, and again, in those circumstances, a bad press may not be a bad thing.

By the same token, it is quite right and proper that journalists and broadcasters should attack even those Christian doctrines that I support. That's democracy, that's diversity. For example, it is not a sign of Armageddon when the Church is attacked for preaching its doctrine on abortion, on sexual morality, or on education. That's the cut and thrust of public debate in a modern, democratic country.

We should not be sitting here today wondering how we should get the Church's opponents off the television and out of the newspapers. We should let that debate happen. And when this period in our national adolescence is over, I think we will hear a more adult kind of debate; with some voices quietly supportive of the Church, and some constructively opposed.

I end with a quote from the Gospel according to Saint John. Christ was telling his followers that they should seek to be recognised not by what they preached, but how they lived:

> By this shall all men know that you are my disciples, if you love one another.
>
> Jn 13:35

I know that I myself have been a beneficiary of the love of Christ, though I have been only a very poor witness to that fact. It is time, ladies and gentlemen, for a larger group than the apostles, the ordained, and the professional messengers, to go forth in their multitudes, and to spread the Good News: that God sent his only begotten Son to live amongst us, and to minister to us. That he so loved the world that he gave us his life, so that we might live forever. He walks amongst us, even now in the person of the humblest curate and the most powerful primate. He is there even in the midst of crisis and scandal.

That's the Good News. Even if it doesn't make tomorrow morning's front page, it can still be passed on, by you and me, in our work, in our daily talk, in our daily witness. Let that daily witness, not some clever marketing strategy, be our most powerful form of persuasion.

PART 3

TOWARDS A WORKING
RELATIONSHIP

THE PRESS AND PRIVACY

John Cunningham

One of the most spectacular cases internationally involving the whole question of privacy and what might not be published, was that of the Duchess of York, Sarah Ferguson. A tabloid ran photographs of her receiving 'financial advice' from her friend. A huge controversy erupted about the topless photographs taken with a long-lens camera during an unsuspecting moment at the poolside in some hideaway that was thought to be private.

On the day they were published – and they added many, many extra copies on to the newspaper sales that particular day – I was interested in the photos. Purely from a professional point of view, you understand!

At the newsagents where I call each morning on my way to the office, I took up a copy of the paper. The girl behind the counter told me that I was the umpteenth person to do that. One of them was a woman, she said, who bought *The Irish Times* each morning and worked in an office nearby. On that morning the woman took up the tabloid with her *Irish Times* and bought the two. And as she was walking out the door of the newsagents she turned with the tabloid in her hand and asked the assistant 'Would you have a paper bag for this?'

The brown paper bag may also explain why some newspapers claim very high circulation indeed, but I'm damned if I ever met someone who admitted reading them.

The title of this section is 'Towards a Relationship that Works.' May I look at this from the perspective of the journalist, the way in which decisions are made, and not so much prescribe how a relationship might work, but try to give an insight into the industry and the way in which it functions, and how it is developing in latter years? It is your business to set about trying to work out 'a working relationship' – though that working title may be a rather coy way of describing something of a crisis of bad publicity which has descended on the Catholic Church in recent years.

I think it would be fair to say that a number of journalists may have the 'brown paper bag' dilemma about some of the material which appears in newspapers and about the direction in which some media would seem to be going. But like all journalists, I too am in the business of selling newspapers. How to strike the balance between 'the public interest' and 'interesting or entertaining to the public' is becoming a bigger and bigger question. Maybe the late Denis Potter, the playwright, put the dilemma at its most extreme when he asked himself if he really wanted to be part of a society where the latest horror video and Michael Jackson record were the news of the day. Ben Bradlee of *The Washington Post* raised the same issue in recent years when he openly questioned where newspapers were going in their bid to match the kind of provocation and shortening span of attention which he felt was being engendered by television.

I speak as a working journalist who daily has to deal with all the pressures and difficulties – and the sheer exhilaration at times – of pursuing a career in journalism. I think it is important in trying to address the issue of a 'working relationship' with any body or organisation, to outline the decision-making processes which are the normal part of journalism, look at a few cases of major stories and maybe then go on to draw some conclusions about what that working relationship might be.

Perhaps I had better explain what I understand 'the public interest' to be. It does NOT mean public curiosity, the need to be diverted, or the need to be entertained. But a journalist, every hour of his or her existence, hovers between 'the good story' and 'the public interest'. Essentially, 'public interest' defined as 'interesting to the public' has always been a part of journalism. I would argue that in many cases, 'the public interest' is becoming more and more defined as the need to entertain and divert the public. It has actually worked well in some areas – the public have been diverted and the media have made money. I am not sure that it has improved newspapers.

In a media market that is becoming increasingly splintered, and competitive – even as it becomes more concentrated in the hands of fewer and fewer people – the pressure to compete is going to continue to grow. We have forecasts of hundreds of television channels. The audiences must come from the same pool of viewers. I would venture to suggest that it is unlikely that higher standards in broadcasting will be the market leader. We had the spectacle a few weeks ago of a major figure on network television in America resigning because a presenter from entertainment was brought in to present a major news programme. The entertainer eventually withdrew ... on this occasion. I can't see many more such victories, in either television or newspapers. For instance, I saw one alarming statistic from the United States recently where the major networks are reported to have dropped their foreign coverage by well over fifty per cent in recent years. Of course, the particular events of the day will have an effect on exactly how much foreign news will be carried, but the opportunity we now have to see some of the satellite channels in this country does show that a number of the major television networks in the United States are pretty inward-looking.

'In the public interest' is loosely defined as the reason the press is said to be in attendance at the courts. It is so that 'justice may be seen to be done'. In other words, the Law invited the Press into the courts so that justice might be seen to be openly and fairly administered. Now such a role is vitally important. I think Nell McCafferty's pioneering coverage of the Dublin District Courts in *The Irish Times* some years ago served to show the courts to the public and may have been instrumental in curbing some of the more exuberant figures on the Bench at the time!

But like every other journalist when I go to the courts, I go because there is a story in it. I would like to think that I go so that justice may be seen to be done. For instance, it was important that *The Connacht Tribune* cover the court hearing of the Brendan O'Donnell murder trial arising out of the murders of Fr Joe Walsh, Imelda Riney and her child. We gave it an average of over two pages of coverage each week during the hearing. It was important, but it also sold newspapers.

Recently we had the Michelle Rocca – Cathal Ryan court case that ran for days and received saturation coverage in all branches of the media. We had colour pieces, comment, photos, summations. The people with the coloured pencils arrived. I heard Vincent Browne on radio one night challenge one of the senior news editors in *The Irish Times* when he was told that it was carrying two full pages as well as a front page story about the trial. What was *The Irish Times* coming to?

Vincent Browne wondered aloud. The sharpish rejoinder was that Vincent Browne might be at exactly the same thing if he was still editor of *The Sunday Tribune!* (And yes, without Vincent Browne in the editorial chair, *The Sunday Tribune* carried major coverage of the trial.)

If this all sounds (on my part) like the old prayer 'Lord, make me good ... but not yet', it is because there really is no easy answer to this dilemma for a journalist. I mean, could anyone seriously suggest that the news editor of a national or provincial paper would decide 'we will carry one shortish report of the Michelle Rocca – Cathal Ryan case'? The news editor could make such a decision. I venture to suggest that he or she might soon find themselves promoted to editing the gardening page as readers flocked to newspapers that carried the details of the trial. There is also the point that it was the parties themselves who brought this issue to the courts and they knew what the scale of the publicity might be likely to be. In other words, that story was already in the public domain, and it was there – in some respects – at the behest of the parties involved. If they wished to produce copy in public that was like an ongoing soap opera, then they should be on their mettle in expecting publicity.

So, on the one hand journalists have the responsibility to be responsible and constructive, but they are also dealing in a market where newspapers have to sell, where reading habits are changing, or dying, where spans of attention may be dictated by a generation raised on television, with what a friend of mine calls the ODTAA rule ... ONE DAMN THING AFTER ANOTHER.

In Ireland the media generally, and newspapers in particular, have had to look at the increasing power of tabloid newspapers in the marketplace. Styles of reporting have changed as people's perception of what they need from their newspapers has changed. For instance, in the recent election campaign, politicians complained loudly that newspapers now rarely cover issues – I presume they mean unemployment, for one. But politicians themselves might be questioned on the whole business of what they now describe as a 'greedy election', in which the campaign seemed for so long to be dominated by the issue of taxation and how much people had in their pockets. Yet in the same breath, they will take credit for running the most controlled and spin-doctor-driven election on record.

There is another element that we should not lose sight of – people do tend to buy the newspapers they want to read. For instance, the morning after *Prime Time* named Charles Haughey as the recipient of the £1.3 million from Ben Dunne, I was staying in a Dublin hotel. The early editions of the newspapers were in the foyer. *The Irish Independent* led with a huge picture and story about Charlie Haughey and the money. *The Irish Times* led with some other story and carried a very short piece inside about Mr Haughey and that money. Was it an accident that they told me *The Irish Independent* was sold out and they had sent out for fifteen more papers, but there were plenty of *Irish Times* left?

We live in a media world where the ground rules are shifting. They are not so much consciously changing as moving almost unnoticed by many. In other words, what is unacceptable or is taken grave exception to today, is commonplace tomorrow. An example of the ground rules changing in which I was directly involved was the reporting of a story on an incident in a Galway boarding school in which the son of a former Government minister was involved. The facts were that he was one of six allegedly involved in an incident; he was suspended after some sort of hearing in the school, and the Gardaí were called in to look into the incident.

Our newspaper reported on the incident on the front page, but we did not give any of the boys' names, or say who they were. I decided, in consultation with the editorial staff, that it would certainly be wrong to name one seventeen-year-old boy, purely because of the fact that his mother was a former minister. We did not know of the hearing that had taken place in the school. I argued also that if we published one name, we should publish all, and that it was insufficient reason to publish the name of one boy allegedly involved in an incident on the basis of who his mother was. In other words, if the boy's mother happened to be just an ordinary, little known, or relatively unknown resident of Galway, then our newspaper certainly would not publish his name.

However, I have to add that because of time schedules, we actually had half an hour in which to make our decision and discuss it. That is almost never the case – typically, in journalism, you have to make instant decisions. And I am not sure that in a few years' time I would make the same decision, because what is by then commonplace in journalism may have moved on substantially. Do the media want to go down that road? How far down that road do they want to go? And is there any discussion on it?

One Sunday newspaper that broke the story, did publish the boy's name and the mother's name in a social diary piece. Its explanation appeared to be that it was a matter of public interest. Two other newspapers which published the names said they did it because the names were already known, having been published by the Sunday newspaper. I would suggest that this could be regarded as a rather strange rationale for a decision.

A recent example of a piece that would certainly be interesting to the public, but of doubtful 'public interest', was the publication of photos and a story of an alleged affair involving a former minister and a 'partner'. I thought the story utterly irrelevant to whether the minister was correct in his dealings with Ben Dunne, or how he ran his ministry in any number of other respects. I would have refused to publish such a story and pictures.

I do not know how many backers I would have in journalism for my line of reasoning. And we got angry letters from readers when I wrote an editorial saying that a minister's life as a minister was open to public scrutiny. One writer criticised us heavily for allegedly being soft on the politicians. It is open season on politicians now and there is huge cynicism out there, but I wondered if an ex-minister's private life should be looked at in this way?

I am not sure that in five years' time I would make the same decision in the cases of either of the two stories I have mentioned above, because by then custom and practice in Irish journalism may have altered pretty dramatically, and my own personal guidelines may have been eroded, or public sensitivities changed.

You see what I mean about the borders being eroded! As what is ordinary or normal in the media changes, as the competition gets tougher and tougher, then the decisions will change. A journalist is bound by the National Union of Journalists' Code of Conduct to respect privacy, ensure that copy is fair and accurate, and does not intrude into grief or distress. But what is acceptable in journalism is changing all the time. And the journalists' view is subjective.

Interestingly, the issue of privacy came up in a major way in the case of the story and photos of a model which appeared in *The Sunday Mirror* – the photos of the model's changing-room were extracted from a video shot secretly from a rooftop. The case was settled, but not before the judge had indicated that he would conduct a separate hearing on breach of the constitutional right to privacy and had given indications of exemplary damages. The case was settled before it could go to hearing, but it will have major implications regarding just how far the media can go on privacy. I think the case was relatively easily judged from a journalistic point of view – it was an appalling way to get photos and a gross invasion of privacy.

This was not the first instance in Irish journalism of a case based on the right to privacy. Some years ago when I was a member of the Broadcasting Complaints Commission we made a decision reprimanding RTÉ because it carried a piece of film footage to illustrate a story on child sex abuse allegations in which it was felt that the child's privacy had been invaded as it was possible to identify the child. That right to privacy existed under the broadcasting legislation.

All these cases were easily decided. Less clear would be the case of a decision to use the name of the Tánaiste's fifteen-year-old son in recording how the Tánaiste was obliged to fly home hurriedly from a summit in Brussels because of a family illness, and to exploit the situation further by trying to find out what was wrong with him. The Tánaiste is a public figure. The fact that he had to fly home is public. But is the son's name and his condition a public property?

To my mind something like the Broadcasting Complaints Commission, or a Press Council, would be an infinitely better way of tackling issues such as privacy or cases of alleged offence by the media, in which there may not be a case strong enough to go to court under our libel or constitutional laws, but where there may be a wrong that should be righted. For instance, that same Broadcasting Complaints Commission found against Gay Byrne and *The Late Late Show* in relation to a programme which was felt to be unfair, on which former minister Seán Doherty was guest. Under the legislation which determines how the Broadcasting Commission operates, stories must be found to be fair to all the interests involved. In fact, surprisingly few cases of complaint succeed because the Commission is very conscious of the rights of the media and the need for a vigorous media.

It is against this sort of media background that the Catholic Church has to consider the business of its working relationship with the media. Perceptions have changed. Society has changed. The stature and status of the Catholic Church has changed. What is relevant has changed.

The Catholic Church has been going through a very difficult time in its history. We have had media spectaculars, for instance, the resignation of Bishop Eamonn Casey.

I was involved in a personal way in covering that story. And it was spectacularly badly handled by the Catholic Church – by whom I mean the clergy and the powers that be. Did people really believe that the story might in some way go away, if Eamonn Casey went to South America? In a world where CNN can do commentary live from a hotel bedroom in Baghdad as the Cruise missiles pass by the hotel windows? There have also been other spectaculars. The Eamonn Casey story is still being spectacularly badly handled because we effectively have a man living abroad on account of a scandal that is now five years old. The man is seventy years of age.

The Church has learned a lot from that time and from other even more painful stories from a Church point of view. The learning process has been slow and painful. But I would think the attitude of the Catholic Church has to be one of something other than a sense of offence and a smouldering distaste for the media. The media do not make up these stories, but they can write them in ways other than how we would like them to appear.

It is not the fault of the media that the Irish Catholic Church for so long concentrated on areas like the Sixth Commandment and is now in difficulties in that area. It is also the misfortune of the Church that these stories are in an area that makes good copy and very readable accounts. But what should be so wonderful about the discovery that priests and religious are men and women also?

The media are simply not going to go away. Warts and all, the media are made up of people who are competent, caring, concerned, committed, campaigning, but they also include people who are incompetent, rushed, less than sensitive. They are a bit like most organisations – including the Catholic Church.

As the *News Of The World* – another one of those newspapers that might come in a brown paper bag – used to say, all human life is there. I think the Catholic Church needs to make a decision to live side-by-side with the media in a professional way.

HOW NOT
'TO LET THE SIDE DOWN'

Colm Kilcoyne

Almost thirty years ago, the editor of a local newspaper in the west of Ireland asked me would I write a weekly column. Only one rule – meet the deadlines. He wished me well.

I had a feeling you were expected to get your bishop's permission to do this kind of thing. Or at least, tell him out of courtesy. So I met the bishop. Now I didn't expect him to throw his arms around me and through tears of joy tell me how he had lived for this day. But neither was I prepared for what he did say. One sentence.

I trust you'll be careful not to let down the side.

Not what you'd call a ringing endorsement. In fact, pretty bleak. But at least, I knew now where I stood.

1. It was clear he saw two sides. There was the Church and there was the media.
2. My place and my job was decidedly with 'our side' and not theirs.

It was a useful moment because it forced me to do some thinking about what kind of backing I'd get if I did write to the secular media, about what kind of Church I belonged to, about how that Church saw its place in society and where the media fitted into all this.

Church documents on the importance of the media

A funny thing, just when my bishop was so nervous of the media, the Catholic Church was saying all kinds of nice things about them. At least since 12 February 1931, when Pope Pius XI pressed a key in a studio on Vatican Hill and inaugurated Vatican Radio, the Catholic Church has signalled its appreciation of the power of the mass media. There are documents galore praising the media and highlighting its potential for evangelisation.

It might be useful to look at some of those declarations of approval. The Vatican Council stated that:

> In our age which is characterised by the mass media, we must not fail to avail of the media for the first proclamation of the message. The Church would feel herself guilty before God if she did not avail of those powerful instruments which human skill is constantly developing and perfecting. (*Evangelii nuntiandi*, 45)

> This Council calls on them [the Church] to remember that they are in duty bound to support and promote media involvement. (*Inter mirifica*, 17)

In 1992, the Catholic Church pulled together many of the strands of the Council documents in a new document called *Aetatis novae*. You'll find here as sophisticated an understanding of the media as you'll find anywhere. Among other observations, this papal document points out that the power of the media is such that not only do they define what issues people will think about, but also how they will think about them:

> Much that men and women know and think about today is conditioned by the media; to a considerable extent, human experience itself is an experience of media. (Par. 2)

Cardinal Martini of Milan has said:

> The media are no longer screens we watch or radios we listen to. They are an atmosphere ... in which we are immersed.... We live in this world of sounds, images, colours, impulses and vibrations as primitive men and women once were immersed in the forest, like fish in water. The media are a new way of being alive. (Cardinal Carlo Maria Martini SJ, *The Hem of Jesus' Garment,* pastoral letter on communications)

So, there is no shortage of understanding of the nature and importance of the media. Why then the Church nervousness and the failure to employ money and talent in their use?

Why was the Irish Church nervous about the media?
We have to look at our recent social and religious history. For most of this century, the Churches held all the cards. The Protestants had *The Irish Times,* the Catholics had *The Irish Independent* and *Irish Press.* Local papers were firmly committed to rocking no boats. Radio was respectful. Critics were oddities or communists or both. The most powerful symbols of identity and the rituals for expressing it were in the hands of the Church. Novenas, devotions, sacred places. The

All-Ireland Finals started with 'Faith of Our Fathers'. The media reflected a respectful Irish society.

Then came the Council, TV, the Beatles, travel bags, the pill, pocket money, free education and, in time, scandals. The old culture of respect was giving way to a culture of questioning. The Council, as we've seen from the quotes, was well aware of the changes and had pleaded that the Church understand and use the media to speak to people moving from the fixed images of the past to the fluid and confusing images of the present.

Its plea had fallen on deaf ears, at least in Ireland. Sure, we had the routinely praised *Radharc* and the Training Centre for radio, television and journalism in Booterstown, but these were mostly seen as the hobby of the restless rather than the essential bread and butter skills of a Church that needed to learn how to dialogue with a newly media-conscious people.

We lost valuable time by not becoming a media-literate Church. This is not as crass as to suggest we should have developed a telephone book of slick speakers at the ready in case the Church needed to be talked out of a tight corner, but that we should have spent time, money and talent learning how to distil the truths of faith into words and images that would translate into media images without either cheapening the content or losing the interest of the receiver.

Instead, we made official the attitude of my ex-bishop. We divided Irish life into sides, ours and theirs. Too often we blamed the media for losing our comfortable place in Irish society. The media may have chronicled the Church's changed status but it is too simple to put the media anywhere near the top of the list of causes.

Changed times presented the Church with two questions
1. What precisely is the nature of the crisis we are going through?
2. What relationship should we have with the media in this evolving society?

A crisis of culture, rather than simply a crisis of faith
I'd suggest that we failed to face both questions. First we ignored the crisis, then we dealt with it as purely a crisis of faith, rather than what it was essentially – a crisis in our culture. The crisis within the Church was part of a wider crisis facing all the institutions of the state. It was not simply the fault of a growing secularism aided and encouraged by a media mainly hostile to the Church. There certainly were elements in the media that took inordinate pleasure in the discomfort of the Church amidst the new order of things, but essentially, the changes had a drive sourced outside the media coverage. The Churches resented the part played by the media in chronicling the crisis – to the extent that we demonised the media. We confused the messenger with the message, identifying the media as a rival, upstart pulpit.

In reality, it was the new way of looking at life, not the media, that challenged all the old institutions. The media, in Cardinal Martini's words, was 'the atmosphere in which we were immersed, facilitating a new way of being alive'. What we should have done, but didn't, was have the faith to believe our own documents. 'In our age, which is characterised by the mass media, we must not fail to avail of the media for the first proclamation of the message' (*Evangelii nuntiandi*, 45).

The most obvious sign of the cultural crisis is what has been called the death of reverence or the end of deference. The shift from authority to experience, from respect to cynicism.

There is a crisis in every institution that is founded on authority, hierarchy and a civil service caste system. These institutions use a language and have expectations of obedience that are out of tune with the times. There is a cynicism in the culture about any institution that projects itself as having an inherited authority.

Ask the British royal family. Ask the Church.

Society no longer agrees on common values

This loss of deference is linked to another change in our culture – the shift from a common language of morality to a glorification of the individual search for meaning. Whether you call it relativism or individualism, the result is a break-up of moral universals. Chat shows and print profiles thrive on people who march to the beat of their own instincts. Orthodoxy appears grey by comparison. In a society where a rainbow of values is seen as more exciting, the Church's monochrome approach to morality lacks lustre. As do the claims of any institution like the Church that preaches a timeless message.

The result is the cult of the lonesome cowboy. The James Dean thing. The death of village culture.

Seamus Heaney has a poem called *'Illo Tempore'* ('At that Time'). He talks about childhood and serving Mass. The comforting world of 'the big missal with the dangled silky ribbons of emerald and purple and watery white'. As altar servers, they 'would assist, confess, receive'.

The poem then moves to adult life. The 'we' of the earlier part has become a solitary 'I'. The comforting world is no more. No silky ribbons of emerald, purple and watery white. Instead the 'I' walks beside the sea, at night, unbearably lonely. This person is not necessarily hostile to Church symbols and language. It may be that they have simply lost meaning.

Like other institutions that nourished and were in turn carried by the village culture, the Church is under pressure. The institution, that is. Bishops, priests, religious – the keepers of the rules and regulations. The power people. The druids. Lay faith is another matter. To some degree it rises and falls with the quality of the leaders. At another, it motors on regardless. Here, I am talking only about the institutional Church.

Church and media scapegoating each other

If the structures of the institution are under pressure, the temptation is to scapegoat others in order to mask the hard questions about oneself. To see transition in terms of sides to be defended rather than a common problem. The Church is part of the culture but sometimes the tendency is to see itself as a victim of the culture.

This was the first reaction to the early sex abuse revelations. To discuss the priests as if they were not part of the priesthood, but aberrations, people whose main crime was that they brought shame on other good-living priests. That was significant in the mess that was made of responding to public and media questions – the problem was seen as individual, not institutional. At times, the institutional figures gave the impression that they resented being quizzed by the media.

To be fair, some media people abuse their power when it comes to covering Church matters. They have chips on their shoulders. A Church scandal or embarrassment is pounced on with such relish that you suspect the energy of the reporting owes more to old scores being settled than to the demands of objective reporting. Unresolved personal history finds a target in the Church.

These few writers do a disservice to themselves, to other reporters and to the Church. They make it easy for the Church to lump all media people and dismiss their work as the product of a peculiar lot. They save the Church from having to take serious criticism seriously.

For the Church to set right its attitudes, it need look no further than its own documents, which ask for an honest, professional, non-fearful engagement with the media.

What kind of relationships should there be between the media and the Churches?

Which brings me to the second challenge – to work out relationships with the media, to see to what extent good manners demands friendship and to what extent the integrity of each demands distance.

I can't remember where I read that what is often lacking in the Church criticism of the media is a matter of emotion and manners, of empathy and professional respect. That much at least.

The Catholic Church, especially, has been bad in developing a professional understanding of the media. We cringe more often than swell with pride when a bishop is being questioned. While I'm at it, I might as well offend the clergy also by saying we priests don't exactly cover ourselves with glory in the presence of the enquiring microphone. Simple things. Like preparation. Like using images and language that say it simply. Like telling the truth. Like understanding that the media have a job to do and they'd like to do it as well as they can. The media and the public ask for little more. They get so much less.

Professional respect. We have some distance to go. An example. A local radio station I know has a notice-board where letters and notes and 'thank you' cards from organisations are pinned up. Thanking presenters for giving coverage to events, thanking them for giving them an interview to get publicity. Some of these come from organisations, some from individuals. In nine years, I've never seen a note from an official Church group thanking me or any other presenter for giving air time. Professional respect!

Local media

And while I am talking local media, could I make a plea for a little accuracy when we use the term 'media'? It covers not just national and Dublin-based media, but local radio and local newspapers. Collectively these outnumber the national media. By and large, they do a decent job. If anything, some of them are too respectful. But they all get tarred with the same suspicious brush.

Of its nature, the media sniffs out what others want to hide. Nicholas Tomalin of *The Sunday Times* was blunt about the job in a piece he wrote some years ago:

> The only qualities essential for real success in journalism are ratlike cunning, a plausible manner, and a little literary ability ... the willingness to betray, if not friends, acquaintances. A reluctance to understand too much too well; an implacable hatred of spokesmen. The capacity to steal other people's ideas and phrases is also invaluable.

So, we are not dealing with angels when we mix with the media. But, let's face it, neither are they when they are dealing with the institutional Church! What it comes down to is realising (to go back to Cardinal Martini) that 'we live in this world of sounds, images, colours, impulses and vibrations as primitive men and women once were immersed in the forest, like fish in water. It is our environment and the media are a new way of being alive'. If this means anything, the Church has an obligation to use the media tools of the day in its work of evangelisation.

Is there a point beyond which Church and media don't mix?

Up to now, I've been pleading for more engagement with the media. However, is there a point beyond which Church and media have to be suspicious of each other? Where they must part company because they are about different things? Where suspicion is healthy?

Avery Dulles, an American Jesuit, identifies six points of tension between the nature of the Church and the priorities of the media. He says that because of these differences in the nature of the Church and of the media, the relationship will be uneasy at times.

> *1. The press is investigative and iconoclastic.* The Church's message is a mystery of faith. A healthy media is profane in the sense that it demands answers to everything in common, logical language. The Church believes that the core of its message occupies a sacred place that is beyond logic. Faith resides in a personal relationship with Jesus Christ, and like any deep relationship is better intuited than expressed.

2. *The media lives off the fresh and the novel. The Church operates in time but its thought frame is eschatological – all is seen in terms of eternity.* Like the bread ad, the media demands today's explanation, today. The Church is happier with a rather broader time-scale.

3. *The Gospel message is one of reconciliation and unity. The media specialises in conflict.* 'Bishop lashes out' is more likely to find space than 'Bishop says his prayers'. The Pope is guaranteed coverage if he attacks modern sexual morality, less sure of column inches if he explores our need for quiet reflection.

4. *The main work of the Church is the spiritual, whereas the media is more at home with the tangible.* More newspapers are sold to people who live in the economy than are sold to people who live in monasteries. That dictates content.

5. *The Church favours uniformity. The media loves the maverick.* Hence the disobedient priest and the dissident theologian will always get notice.

6. *Church teaching is often complex and subtle. The media wants stories that are simple and striking.* The Trinity is less amenable to catchy headlines than is a shoot-out on O'Connell Street.

This analysis by Avery Dulles is useful. It alerts us to the fact that the Church and the media can hold hands only for so long. There comes a point where they each are about different things, have a different perspective and trade in different realities. That is true.

But his list could also create problems if it were to be taken as an excuse for non-engagement with the media. None of the opposites that he sets up in his list is absolute. Some simplify the roles of Church and media to the point where his analysis loses value. The media isn't quite so functional and the Church isn't so otherworldly as Dulles suggests. His observations are most helpful when they warn the Church against believing that all it needs is good PR.

It is not about PR. No, the Church is essentially about the mystery of God's revelation of himself in the person of Jesus Christ. That mystery has been given into the care of what are at times grubby hands. The hands should be open to media inspection. The transcendent nature of the mystery is, literally, another story.

In the heel of the hunt, the Church is a family on a journey. At different times and different places this family has articulated its pilgrimage by whatever images and language were to hand. In our time, we have an explosion of images and language. That is both a challenge and an opportunity.

We are called as Church to use all the richness of creation and creativity to alert each other to the presence of the Incarnate Word; called to introduce to each other the Word made flesh and the hungers of the heart; to mate the desire for happiness with the richness of the Gospel.

Brian Friel says it all in *Philadelphia, Here I Come*. The young Garr is fleeing the constipation of Irish life for what he imagines is the freedom of the big city. His anger is with life and the Church that claims to interpret it. The canon comes in to offer words of wisdom to the young man, to warn him about the dangers out there to his immortal soul.

In frustration Garr screams at the deaf ears of the canon:

> You could translate all this loneliness,
> this dreadful bloody buffoonery,
> into Christian terms that will make life bearable to us all.
>
> Why arid, Canon? Isn't this your job, to translate?
> Why don't you speak then?

The Churches' job is to translate the Gospel and our hungers into a common language. Rarely can people have lived in a world where the means of creating this common language were greater than they are now. The media, in all its forms, is a huge colouring-box from which to create a landscape that will bring us to the edge of the mystery. 'Much that men and women know and think about today is conditioned by the media. To a considerable extent, human experience itself is an experience of the media' (*Aetatis novae,* 2).

Finally, that bishop who underwhelmed me with affirmation back when I started writing for newspapers eventually retired. From the day he did, he became my biggest fan. Never failed to comment on the articles. Told me how much he appreciated them. Once free of the burden of office, he could be himself. There is both a message and some hope there.

THE RELIGIOUS JOURNALIST

Andy Pollak

This has been a good week for the media. We can justly feel a
certain sense of self-congratulation for the role we played – or
rather fine journalists like Sam Smyth of *The Sunday
Independent* and Matt Cooper of *The Sunday Tribune* played
– in the uncovering of the appalling 'golden circle' inhabited
by the likes of Ben Dunne, Charlie Haughey, Michael Lowry
and the other leading Irish citizens who hold millions of
pounds in undeclared, untaxed 'offshore' bank accounts.

Such smugness is usually bad for the soul. So I'm going to
disturb it this morning by talking about the many
shortcomings of my profession of journalism in an effort to
demystify it a little and in the interests of necessary self-
criticism and provocative debate.

At its best the media should provide and embody what the
Belgian Jesuit Jan Kerkhofs calls the most positive aspects of
contemporary liberalism: the promotion of human rights,
opposition to racial discrimination, women's emancipation,
respect for those of all religions and none, the peace
movement, and, in general terms, the recognition of human
dignity and the rejection of every form of totalitarianism.

Without the liberal values of freedom of conscience,
opinion and expression, respect for diversity, rejection of
totalitarianism and as free a flow of ideas as a society of
powerful vested interests will allow, the job of informing

people about the events which shape their lives would be impossible.

The profession of journalism at its best, therefore, should aim to bring the light of publicity to bear on those holding power, wealth and authority so as to make them more answerable for their actions to the public, or rather the more or less representative section of it who constitute newspaper readers. I will be referring in this paper largely to the media as represented by daily newspapers, rather than the much more powerful electronic media of radio and television, with which I am much less familiar.

In fact the media, like all our flawed human institutions, rarely lives up to these high ideals – and I say this as someone who tries to have a broad, liberal view of the world; is a passionate believer in the centrality to civilised society of freedom of speech and expression; is left-of-centre in politics; and a member of a small, liberal non-conformist Church.

Our newspapers reflect the liberalism of those who run and write in them, as well as many who read them. Editors and journalists on Irish papers are overwhelmingly drawn from the urban middle class and share that class's concern with material prosperity and individual freedoms.

Similarly they share the mild – and sometimes not so mild – anti-clericalism of many middle-class people. Editors and senior journalists tend to be from the generation which came of age in the 1960s and early 1970s, and who have reacted strongly against the rigid adherence to a narrow Catholic orthodoxy imposed on them in their youth by parents, priests and teachers.

Because of the continuing broad adherence to Catholic worship and values, and the historical identification of Catholicism with the nation, this anti-clericalism does not take on an organised political form, but manifests itself in an indifference to organised religion and some antagonism towards Catholic authority figures, notably conservative bishops and priests.

I have to say that I have detected an increase in media anti-clericalism in recent years. I first felt it strongly after the Brendan Smyth child sex abuse scandal broke three years ago. There was an unspoken assumption that for the moment, at any rate, it was open season on the Catholic Church and its bishops. This mood was exacerbated by the Church's apparent inability to understand and empathise with the level of public anger about the horrific things being done to children by a small number of paedophile priests. The Church's slowness to respond and the defensive nature of its statements when it did respond – plus its failure to communicate its concern through the media – did not help.

When this anti-clerical atmosphere was at its height, I felt I was being something of a deviant if I put in a good word for the Church among my fellow journalists. I found it difficult for a period to interest my editors in any religious topic other than the ramifications of the latest twist in the clerical child sex abuse scandal. And if it was like that in *The Irish Times,* how much more extreme must have been the situation in the tabloid papers.

I agree with Bishop Willie Walsh that this has little to do with anything as coherent and worked-out as a media conspiracy to undermine the Church's influence. It has much more to do with two quite different factors. The first of these is what my colleague Fintan O'Toole calls 'the three-minute culture'. 'If the media does not treat well of theology and Christian spirituality, neither does it treat well of any intellectual problem or any non-Christian notion of spirituality. The demands of a three-minute culture are not the enemy of the serious treatment of religion alone', he has written.

The attention span of a daily newspaper editor or journalist tends to be twenty-four hours. What he or she is interested in is what is happening today for publication in tomorrow's paper. Any social, intellectual or cultural trend which demands a longer attention span is usually dismissed as being not newsworthy. The long-term trends in Northern Ireland, for example, are rarely discussed, even after Tony Blair's first keynote speech in Belfast six weeks ago when he said that no one in his audience was likely to see Northern Ireland as anything but a part of the UK in their lifetimes.

Did this lead to a ferment of articles about what it might mean for the long-term strategy of Republicanism and Unionism? Or about the renewed possibility of a new accommodation between moderate Unionists and moderate Nationalists? Or about the significance of the demographic changes in Northern Ireland, with Protestants moving from south and west to north and east and Belfast becoming a Nationalist city? Or what will happen to the North's economy if the current 'semi-ceasefire' continues indefinitely and both Whitehall and Westminster begin to lose interest? I'm an avid North-watcher and I didn't see any of these crucial subjects dealt with, even in my own heavyweight newspaper.

On the other hand, when something newsworthy is deemed to have happened, we witness what the BBC director-general John Birt calls a 'feeding frenzy', in which the wider public interest is often lost sight of. Politicians and journalists become endlessly obsessed with the daily minutiae of the current controversy: in recent years I can think of a number of examples – the events surrounding the fall of the Albert

Reynolds Government and, in my own area, the endless speculation about the misdeeds of the absent Bishop Comiskey. The result is that the story is turned into a kind of 'national soap opera' while the deeper political and moral issues go unexplored.

It does not help that so many journalists come from similar social backgrounds. This is not exactly the 'Dublin 4' uniformity which paranoid rural conservatives love to hate. But certainly the important people in D'Olier Street, Abbey Street and at Montrose tend to live in middle-class south Dublin.

In this deeply class-divided city, with middle-class and working-class people living almost entirely separate existences, our editorial executives and senior journalists rarely have to see how the people of west Tallaght, north Clondalkin, Ballymun or Darndale live. The vast majority of *Irish Times* journalists, for example – myself included – live in a triangle bordered by Dublin Bay, the Grand Canal and a line from Dún Laoghaire to Templeogue. If we don't know our own poor and working-class neighbours, how much less will we know about the strange 'traditional' Catholics of rural Ireland?

The people who own and edit newspapers belong to the establishment, and will inevitably seek to produce newspapers that will buttress the status quo which serves them so well. Irish journalists in the 1990s, with a few noble exceptions – Veronica Guerin is the obvious one – are rarely allowed by the editors to uncover the real abuses or scandals among the powerful in any systematic way. We too have become part of the establishment.

The weight of sociological evidence is that 'the media are, if anything, biased against change, and tend, whether by action or omission, to promote the interests of those with greater economic or political power in society'. Those people, he adds, include the bishops.

The Irish media, like the Irish Catholic Church, is also notoriously anti-intellectual, although my own paper occasionally has a valiant stab at changing this. The daily news, the latest row, the clash of politicians and paramilitaries, are our bread and butter.

Newspapers loudly proclaim that a free press is an essential element in any healthy democracy, and of course they are right. But people should not get the impression that the press or broadcasting organisations are themselves run on democratic lines.

We all know about the huge monopolistic power of press barons like Rupert Murdoch and Tony O'Reilly. However, inside newspapers and broadcasting organisations there is also something of the atmosphere of a medieval court, with the editor (or director-general) – provided he or she keeps the readership (or viewing figures) high – having something of the infallible aura of a medieval monarch. When he or she expresses an opinion, scores of middle-management acolytes scurry to do, or even anticipate, his or her bidding.

It is one of our journalistic articles of faith that we write for a public which has 'the right to know'. In fact I can tell you, as a journalist of twenty-five years' experience, that we write primarily for our editors. If the 'sun king' is pleased with our work, we are content.

Let me make a few suggestions about how the Irish Catholic Church might go about improving its message on the eve of the twenty-first century and how it might better use the media in the process.

Firstly, it has to accept that the media – and especially

television – is a growing power in the contemporary world, and learn how to use it, rather than constantly bemoaning its faults. It has to face up to the perhaps unpalatable truth that the power of the pulpit is gone forever, to be replaced by the extraordinary power of the magic tube in the corner of the living-room.

That's going to be very difficult for a Church which has wielded such enormous power and influence in this country over the past 150 years. Power is the ability to make people afraid. As recently as thirty or forty years ago Catholic Irish people were afraid of the power of the bishop or the parish priest. It was unthinkable to criticise either of them in public, let alone in print, and many people thought it unlucky even to criticise them in private. They had God's all-powerful legions behind them, and lots of friends in high political places. The threat of hell was their ultimate weapon.

Now people are far less afraid of the Catholic Church. You don't lose your job if you criticise the Church these days, except perhaps in the odd school. You don't lose your friends, or your community, except perhaps in some more traditional rural areas. In the wake of the clerical sex abuse scandals, priests and bishops – up to and including the Cardinal Archbishop of Armagh – were publicly challenged, criticised and even, on occasion, insulted. Journalists now interrogate bishops on behalf of a public which has 'the right to know', in itself a clear sign of their waning powers.

The Church has to realise that it is now in the market-place, competing with other religious and political organisations to get its message across via the most powerful communication tool in human history, television, and the fantastic worldwide electronic networks which service both television and the press. Increasingly, if a group with a message does not get on those networks, that message goes unheard.

The electronic pulpit is there to be used, as some of the dreadful right-wing religious television stations in the US have shown. The age of the sound bite is with us, whether we like it or not (and I don't), and priests and bishops have to dispense with their sermons when it comes to addressing a mass public and learn how to become masters of that sound bite.

I'm being serious. Look at the way in which Father Seán Healy of CORI* has turned himself into a master user of the Irish media. Five years ago he was seen by many, particularly in RTÉ, as another worthy, rather long-winded seller of a difficult message – the need to tackle the problem of poverty in Ireland. Now, through his assiduous study of how the media works and the superb presentation of his campaign materials – his press releases are a model of how to present a complex subject in an eye-catching way – he is a regular on TV and radio panels on politics and the economy and, largely as a result of this, is having a significant influence on Government thinking.

A more general point, made better by others, is the crying need for a leadership in the Irish Church which is not afraid of the modern world. Both the people and the media love a leader like Bishop Willie Walsh because he is straight-speaking, easy to understand and courageous in dealing with modern problems like marriage breakdown. Young people in particular, with their quickness to spot hypocrisy in their elders, value and will listen to such an honest and outspoken leader.

* Conference of Religious of Ireland

The Irish Church, as the recent survey of Dublin priests showed*, desperately needs such leaders. And the media also values such people – look at the way the Italian media (and as a result, the Italian people) have taken Cardinal Martini of Milan to their hearts, or – in a more complex way, in a scandal-ridden society like the US – the American media found Cardinal Bernardin of Chicago such an attractive figure.

The Church can learn how to use the media when it has leaders like this in charge. Look at how the American Catholic hierarchy – again led by Bernardin – set the agenda in the debate preceding the 1990 Gulf War, so that Protestant clergy and politicians alike found themselves discussing the morality of armed conflict in Catholic terms of what constituted a 'just war'. Look at the considerable impact the English and Welsh bishops' document *The Common Good* had in the run-up to the last British election (compare the extraordinary fact that the Irish hierarchy did not publish its excellent letter on unemployment, *Work is the Key,* until *AFTER* the 1992 Irish election was over).

Father Dermod McCarthy, who spoke to you yesterday, has written of the striking contrast between the relaxed, shirt-sleeved Brazilian bishops meeting the international press and the nervous, often mutually hostile atmosphere when a frightened bishop is sent out to face the media after a meeting of the hierarchy at Maynooth.

Because of the deep conservatism of the present Pope and his Curia, most of the really outstanding potential leaders of the Irish Church – men like Enda McDonagh, Seamus Ryan, Oliver Crilly and Dermot Lane (many of them also superb

---

* Reading the Signs of the Times, A Survey of Priests in Dublin, Dublin: Veritas, 1997

communicators) – have been passed over when it came to appointing bishops.

Some obvious questions must also be asked. Why do we so rarely hear from our religious leaders at times of intense national debate over political moral issues – apart from, of course, the old faithfuls of abortion and divorce? Where was the Church during the nasty outbreak of anti-refugee paranoia during the election (in which some sections of the media contributed to the unsavoury atmosphere)? Where is the Church when our political and business leaders are corrupting the body politic with their lying and cheating and dodging taxes on unbelievable sums of money sloshing around in offshore bank accounts?

Yesterday's *Morning Ireland* featured a smooth-spoken accountant who refused to accept that any corruption was taking place. Why not a bishop to tell us in clear, unambigious terms that what the McCracken Tribunal is uncovering is downright dishonest, immoral, and even – to use an old-fashioned word – wicked.

While on the subject of the sins of big business, I believe – and I speak here as someone who calls himself a socialist – that the Catholic Church internationally has a huge opportunity at the moment, following the collapse of communism and the discrediting of the socialist model of society, to become the real champion of the poor, the unemployed, the hopeless, the marginalised – to espouse the 'theology of liberation' and mount a powerful Christian critique of the excesses of international capitalism.

It won't happen, of course. The Church in most countries is far too tied in with the ruling classes to even contemplate such a cataclysmic step. It will continue instead to hide behind the brave, individual work of people like Peter

McVerry, Seán Healy, the environmental activist Seán McDonagh and Sister Stan Kennedy, without, of course, ever giving them any real power by making them bishops.

I'm going to end with a plea for a little mutual humility between Church and media. It has been the cataclysm of the clerical sex abuse scandals which has taught the Irish Catholic Church to start saying sorry for its mistakes. I applaud Willie Walsh for doing the same over the running sore of Irish inter-Church relations, the *Ne Temere* decree, and, as a Protestant Irishman, I am sorry for the begrudging response his statement received among some Church of Ireland elements.

But we in the media also need to learn a little humility. Until recently, newspapers and broadcasting organisations rarely if ever apologised unless forced to do so by the threat of legal action. Corrections to incorrect reports (and there are plenty of those in Irish newspapers) are hidden away at the bottom of an inside page instead of being given the size and space equivalent to the original article and headline.

There is a completely misplaced sense of solidarity among Irish journalists, so that you rarely hear them criticise each other in public or in print, however justified (how many journalists did you hear criticising the Irish media for their irresponsible, sensationalist coverage of the refugees issue during the recent election? – Fintan O'Toole and Vincent Browne were honourable exceptions). There is not the remotest sign of any Press Council-type media watchdog body on the horizon.

I was talking earlier about the Church having lost its power to frighten people. Some might say the growing power of the media – particularly to invade people's privacy at difficult and painful moments in their lives – is frightening. I know that if any of my family or friends were in any kind of trouble that was about to become the object of media attention, I would warn them to be very careful about which journalist they talked to (preferably only to a journalist they know and could trust, or one who came recommended by someone they knew and could trust). Really trustworthy journalists – perhaps like trustworthy people in most professions – are in the minority, I'm afraid.

So let us, as two powerful and not very accountable elements in Irish society, recognise our own faults as well as each other's. Maybe that would be as good a point as any to start building a better relationship between us in the future.

INEVITABLE TENSION

Vincent Browne

I hope you can endure what I have to say as presented in good faith by somebody who is outside your Churches, who has been a journalist for a long time and comes to this issue from the perspective of a journalist and a former editor.

The role of the media: adversarial *vis-à-vis* institutions of power

Media has a role in democracy, certainly not as important a role as the media professes it to be but it is none the less important to hold institutions of power accountable to society as a whole. Institutions of power are in the main the government of the day, the politicians and the Dáil, the Garda Síochána, trade unions, big business. Inevitably, in holding these institutions of power accountable, an adversarial relationship exists or evolves between the media and the institutions. And invariably the institutions or the people who populate them perceive the media as being anti-them, as being outside their culture, unable to communicate the essence of what they are about and being unsympathetic to their purpose. I have found this particularly in relation to the Gardaí, who are deeply resentful of any questioning of their role. The media is to a very large extent the cipher of the Gardai; and so much of the crime reporting that goes on is merely a faithful regurgitation of briefings from Garda officers. But in so far as the media has reported, for instance, the abuses of power in relation to Garda brutality, this has been greatly resented by the Garda Síochána.

I recall, for instance, how a major scandal occurred within the Garda Síochána back in the 1970s in relation to fingerprinting. It arose after the murder of the British Ambassador in 1976 when a helmet found near the scene of the murder was examined for fingerprints. The officer who initially examined it found no fingerprints on it. It was subsequently examined by the head of the fingerprint section in the Garda Síochána, who discovered a fingerprint on the helmet and subsequently identified it as that of the person who been suggested to him as the likely suspect. On examination of this by the officer who originally examined the helmet he found there were no similarities between the two fingerprints. A dispute arose within the Garda Síochána which went on for several months, until eventually it was discovered that the fingerprint on the helmet was that of the Garda who originally examined the helmet and on disposing of the helmet had left the fingerprint on it.

An investigation by the head of the fingerprint section of Scotland Yard found that the scandal was such as to endanger the science of fingerprinting world-wide. You can all guess what happened: the officers who had identified the scandal were demoted and those responsible for the scandal were promoted. I tell this story merely as an instance of how deeply the Gardaí resented the media investigation of what went on and very often put it about that the journalists were motivated by sympathy with the Provisional IRA, or whatever.

That kind of tension between large, powerful institutions and the media is commonplace. I say this because it partly explains, I believe, the tension that very often exists between the Catholic Church and the media. It isn't all because the media is anti the Catholic Church.

The power of the Catholic Church

The Catholic Church does exercise enormous power in society. It exercises great political and cultural power. It is hugely conditioning. Because such a large proportion of the population are adherents of the Catholic Church, the minds of the people in this society have been conditioned by the Church, politically as well as religiously, socially, culturally and lots of other ways. Independently of that the Church has exercised enormous political power and I will deal with that in a moment. The Catholic Church is also a very powerful financial institution. Its revenues are huge by any standards in this society, probably larger than those of any but the largest corporations in the state. It has huge property wealth and exercises considerable financial clout. In addition, of course, it has great power in the educational sphere through its control of a large segment of our educational institutions. And, of course, it also has enormous power in the health sphere through its control of hospitals. So, inevitably and unavoidably, a tension will be there between the media and this hugely powerful institution in society, independent of any agenda the media itself might be running.

It there weren't a tension between the media and the Catholic Church there would be something wrong with the media! I'm saying this not because there is anything intrinsically wrong with the Catholic Church but simply because that adversarial relationship needs to be there for accountability to operate. The Catholic Church reacts more fiercely to attempts to hold it accountable than do other institutions. Other institutions, for instance the judiciary, are prickly about any attempt to hold them accountable. They resent the suggestion that we would want to examine the ideological predilections of judges, so that we might then know how they reach decisions on major issues, what canons of constitutional interpretation or statutory interpretation they might employ. There is great resentment within the legal profession generally to any such suggestion, to any outside intrusion. You may remember a few years ago the fuss there was over the wig issue. The members of the Bar went literally berserk at the idea that they would be required to dispose of their wigs and to operate in a manner respectful of the equality between them and the people before the courts – and they won in the end. But the point I'm making is that while institutions are naturally prickly about attempts to hold them accountable, I think the Catholic Church is more so than other institutions. And it is so, I believe, because of the tradition of the Church which has not allowed any space for accountability at all. The Church, in its authoritarian hierarchical structure, isn't sympathetic to the idea of being answerable for the exercise of its enormous power.

The political power of the Catholic Church
Returning to the issue of the Catholic Church's political power, we could trawl the pages of history to illustrate it; obviously the issue of the Mother and Child Scheme of forty-six years ago would immediately come to mind. I would just ask you to remember that in the Dáil debate that followed every TD who spoke, bar Peadar Cowan, acknowledged the right of the Catholic hierarchy to determine issues of morality such as the issue of morality at stake in the mother and child affair. It is staggering that the question of whether the state should make free provision for the care of mother and newly-born child, and to do so on a non-means-tested basis, could have been a moral issue.

One could easily argue that opposition to it could be a

moral issue, but that support for it could be a moral issue is nowadays quite staggering. But that is not now the matter I want to allude to. It is the acceptance at the time by every TD who spoke in the Dáil, including Dr Noel Browne, that the Catholic hierarchy had an absolute right to determine these moral issues and that that determination would be binding on Catholic representatives in the Dáil, and, because we were a Catholic state, on the state as a whole. Of course the line has softened since then and political influence and power are exercised by the Catholic Church somewhat more subtly nowadays.

In 1976 when Paddy Cooney, not quite a liberal, introduced the liberalising legislative measures on contraception, he was defeated because the then Taoiseach and the then Minister for Education voted against their own Government. The Catholic Church's pronouncement attempted to dictate to the Catholic members of the Dáil how they should vote on that issue and did so crudely and in the same voice they had deployed in 1951.

But it's changed since then. In the recent controversies on contraception, divorce and homosexual law reform there has been a shift of ground by the Catholic Church. That has been achieved through the deployment of the notion of the common good. It is argued that divorce, for instance, ought to be opposed, not because it's contrary to the teachings of the Catholic Church but because it's contrary to the common good. But of course that is the perception of the common good from a Catholic perspective and it is only another means of arguing the point that the teachings of the Catholic Church ought to be enshrined in legislation or that the opposite should not occur.

The Church and social justice

But quite apart from that I believe that the Church has exercised political power perhaps more significantly through its influence on our political culture. The anti-democratic tendencies in Irish society owe their origins in part to the Catholic culture which is essentially anti-democratic itself. A certain elitism and class distinction has derived from Catholic culture too. I went to Castleknock College, which was an elitist school and never in my time was it ever drawn to my attention or the attention of the other students that we were in a privileged position in society and that we owed that privilege not to anything inherent in ourselves but purely through the circumstances of fortune and birth. We were not told that society was unfair in the distribution of resources on the basis of such arbitrary contingencies. Neither were we told that we owed a duty of redistribution of wealth and power to people less privileged than ourselves. That was never the ethos of the schools that I went to. Nor do I believe was it ever the ethos of the other posh schools around the country – Clongowes, Newbridge, Roscrea, Rockwell, Belvedere, Blackrock College, and all the posh convents. That was never the ethos of those schools and, nowadays, as far as I can perceive it, I don't believe that is the ethos of those schools today. This attitude has had a powerfully conditioning influence on society as a whole. Among Catholics who wield power their religious education has imbued if not quite a disdain, a neglect of considerations of social justice. I think that has been a significant factor.

I think that the Catholic Church has contributed culturally to the elitism and the absence of social justice, more particularly to the absence of concern for social justice that exists in large parts of society. I know that people respond: Did

I read the statements of the bishops whenever it was to do with the dignity of work? Am I not aware of the work done by CORI? Am I not aware of the statements made by Archbishop Connell recently and by Bishop Murray in Limerick? But can anyone here really put their hand on their heart and say the Catholic Church has stood out prominently, forcefully, vigorously and courageously for social justice in this society and used their power and their influence in the same way they have sought to do it in relation to other issues? Manifestly, they have not. You will find stridency and vigour in the tone of the statements by the Catholic hierarchy on abortion and divorce referenda over the past several years. They have sought a prominence for them and they have read them in Churches and they have made sure they have widespread publicity and distribution for them throughout society.

The Catholic Church has in the main, in keeping with its tradition down through the years, been the supporter if not the agent of social injustice. In its focus on the other-worldliness and the afterlife there is in its thrust not quite an indifference but a playing down of the demands of social justice generally.

In the time I was growing up and since then I have never heard a priest or a bishop speak out against the gross injustice in the treatment of servant boys and girls in rural Ireland. No doubt somebody is going to be able to refer me to a statement made in 1927 by some bishop in the West of Ireland. But in general, can you say the Church stood by and attempted to address the gross abuse of power by farmers, by shopkeepers, by creamery managers and others in their social relations with people they called, viewed as and treated as their servants? I think any of us who have read *Angela's Ashes* will appreciate the chill and the numbness it conveys. I certainly had a sense of anger that such a level of poverty and humiliation and degradation could go on in the city near where I lived and amidst significant wealth and extravagance. And again, the Catholic Church did not seem to speak out against it, and to some extent were the agents of that injustice.

The Catholic Church and women
But perhaps the most significant influence of the Catholic Church culturally and politically is in relation to women.

Look at the condescension of the Church nowadays, towards women. We are constantly reminded how much women are involved in all levels of the Church; how they are consulted and how they have become part of the ministry of the Church, right up to but not quite to the priesthood; how they have enormous influence in schools and how they are respected and all the rest. All this seemingly is meant to show how important women are in the Church. The fact is that is just adds insult to injury and it continues the injustice done to women by the Catholic Church over the centuries. It is not so long ago since there was a practice of 'churching' women who had given birth. Just think of the mindset that had given rise to that practice. There is no bishop getting up and expressing apology or expressing regret over this and saying 'Oh God, I don't know why we did it, and it's awful and let's try to undo the harm that was done to women in the past and the influence we had on cultural attitudes towards women.' If the Church treats women in the way that it has done and still does, how can the rest of society, hugely conditioned by the Catholic Church, treat women fairly? The utter incomprehension on the part of the Catholic Church of the arguments on the pro-choice side in the abortion debate should not be surprising. There is no understanding that perhaps it isn't always morally wrong for a woman who has been brutally raped, who is deeply traumatised by the pregnancy, who is driven to the pitch of madness by the thought of having to bring that pregnancy to full term, to choose to abort that innocent human. She didn't have any choice in that innocent human coming into being. Why should the agencies of state be used to require her, irrespective of the trauma imposed and inflicted on her, to bring it to full term? I know the slippery slope argument in relation to abortion and I'm repelled by the lunchtime abortion recently announced in England, but I'm simply reflecting on the incomprehension of the Catholic Church of the view that perhaps that it isn't always morally wrong for a woman to make the choice in her own circumstances and in her own life as to what should be done with her body.

I think that a lot of the language used by the Catholic Church and by others is essentially deeply disrespectful of the autonomy of women.

The accountability of the Catholic Church
In so far as the media has attempted to hold the Church accountable with regard to these issues it is right that it does so. I would actually be critical of the media for not doing so more comprehensively and more consistently. Again I mention the huge financial power of the Church, which it holds with almost no accountability. I know someone is going to tell me about how diocesan accounts are now published. But what facility exists for enquiry into the use of the funds that are available to the dioceses?

Take the disposal of property by the Catholic Church. Again, what responsibility is exercised in respect of that? And how did the Church acquire this very considerable wealth? It acquired it from the people of this society in the main. Surely there is some obligation of accountability arising from that?

Scandal and the Catholic Church

This brings me on to the scandals affecting the Church in the recent past. I will divide the scandals into two sections: those relating to perceived hypocrisy on the part of Church leaders and the issue of paedophilia. With regard to the issue of perceived hypocrisy, this is the issue with which the media has been most obsessed. I think that it is the issue of least significance. How is it significant that among all the bishops that we have known down the years, that one bishop has a child and goes to America to avoid embarrassment? How is that significant? Isn't it the wonder that it hasn't happened much more often! Of course there is an element of hypocrisy involved in that bishop preaching chastity and responsibility and whatever. But aren't we all hypocrites, don't we all profess principles and values which we fail to live up to? That to me seems to be an issue of almost no consequence.

Similarly, with regard to the Fr Michael Cleary issue, I cannot see that it has any consequence at all. And the fact that he may have been a hypocrite and I stress *may*, I think you're saying nothing about him that you cannot say of me and of most people that I know. So I think the media focus on that has been to a large extent prurient.

On the issue of paedophilia, there has been a mistaken focus on the part of the media. It is not significant that a certain number of priests and other clerics have been involved in the sexual abuse of children. This happens throughout society generally and it would be surprising if in the group of people who comprise the clergy there weren't people guilty of paedophilia. I don't find that troubling, except perhaps to wonder whether the prevalence of paedophilia among celibate clergy has some tenuous connection with the issue of celibacy. I cannot but wonder if enforced celibacy hasn't a dysfunctional effect. Those who dismiss that possible connection are mistaken. What I do find disturbing has been the reaction of the Catholic hierarchy. If you look closely at the statements made by the bishops who have had to deal with the issue, it is evident that the statements are made on the evidence of legal advice. That legal advice has focused on the question of vicarious liability, whether the Church itself as an institution or the diocese itself could be sued by the victims. The focus on that is evident in all the statements made by the bishops in relation to paedophilia. I think it's simply obscene.

The Church and political attitudes in society
The Church, in its role in society generally, must wonder about its contribution to the political attitudes that are now so prevalent in society. The frenzy over crime is something that has been deeply disquieting, arising, as it has, from no objective valid evidence whatsoever. The crime rate is lower now than it was in 1983. The incidence of serious crime it is down, as are crimes against the person. And yet we have had this frenzy over crime which is basically an impulse to lock up people who express their alienation from society by committing crimes, mainly against property. The focus on crime is evidence of a meanness in society as a whole. The media has, of course, contributed hugely to this itself and, in my view, RTÉ particularly has contributed greatly to this culture which I think is regressive and regrettable.

I have to acknowledge there are serious problems with

regard to the media itself and to monopolies in the media. There are agendas within the media which are certainly not representative of values shared throughout society. And I think that there is a legitimate concern on the part of people in religious communities and Churches about the fact that the media, which is now verging towards monopolistic, does not share or reflect the values which many of you do. That's true not just of you but of many other sections of society.The agenda of the poorer sections of society is one that is entirely ignored and neglected by the media.

There is a problem of access to the media by all those people who are not part of the agenda of the media, and although the letters columns are somewhat open and it is possible for outsiders to get a look in now and again, basically the essential thrust of the media is one dictated by its own agendas, not by the varying and often contradictory agendas of society as a whole. That has to be addressed.

PART 4

THE FREEDOM OF THE RELIGIOUS PRESS

OWNERSHIP AND RESPONSIBILITY

David Quinn

We are fortunate enough to live in a country where freedom of the press is pretty much taken for granted. Journalists do not operate within a regime where they are subject to direct censorship by Government. This is not a totalitarian regime.

Nevertheless, even in democratic societies, freedom of the press, including the religious press, can be circumscribed in a number of ways. I will list some of them. In doing so I will try to demonstrate that freedom of the press is the product of a fairly complex matrix of forces. Finally, I will deal with the importance of a free religious press in a society increasingly indifferent to religion.

One way in which press freedom can be compromised is through direct intervention by the owner or the trustees. Sometimes this intervention is justified. I will come to that. At other times, however, intervention is entirely unacceptable and violates every canon of press freedom.

Recently there has been considerable public controversy surrounding allegations that a sweetheart deal had been arranged between Fianna Fáil and Independent Newspapers whereby the editorial weight of the group would be put behind Fianna Fáil in exchange for certain concessions favourable to the wider business interests of the owner.

In so far as this is true, it is an example of how a newspaper can be compromised by business dealings which have nothing directly to do with the paper itself.

Then there is the matter of owners or trustees directing an editor to take a certain stance on a particular issue. This is to be differentiated from what I have just outlined. In this case the intervention is not motivated by a desire to secure a commercial advantage, but rather by a view of what the publication is all about, i.e. what it stands for. For example, if the publication is traditionally left-of-centre, then the owners or trustees may want to see their publication support a given public-spending programme which, to date, for whatever reason, has been overlooked.

Whether or not this presents the editor with a problem depends of course on whether or not the editor agrees with the stance he or she is being forced, or encouraged, to take. If he or she agrees with the stance, then there is no problem, although it could be argued that a dangerous precedent has been set. The way has been paved for future interference.

If the editor does not agree with the stance being forced upon him, then he or she is faced with a choice between acquiescence or resignation, no easy decision for someone who is probably facing a mortgage payment at the end of month. The question which arises at this point of course is, does the owner of a newspaper have the right to interfere, intervene, direct, influence – use whichever word you will – in the editorial decisions of the newspaper?

If the answer is 'No', then apart from commercial reasons, why would someone wish to own a newspaper at all? Legendary newspaper owners such as Lord Beaverbrook of *The Daily Express* would have seen no sense at all in owning a newspaper they could not influence. They bought their newspapers, or they founded their newspapers specifically with the aim of influencing public opinion.

It would never have occurred to an owner such as Lord Beaverbrook to appoint an editor whose views were not more or less aligned with his own. The same applies to trustees. Trustees will only appoint an editor whose views will further the aims of the trust with which they are charged. In such a scenario a fundamental disagreement will simply not arise between editor and owner or editor and trustee.

It is, as I have outlined, a different matter if the owner is being influenced not by his or her political outlook, but by his or her own commercial interests.

What applies in the wider world of newspapers applies also in the world of religious publications. If a publication is owned by the hierarchy, or a diocese, or a religious order, then the owners will presumably wish that their publication roughly adheres to their line. If not, if the publication is taken in a contrary direction, then the owners would have good cause to wonder why they should bother to continue their involvement at all.

In what other ways can press freedom be curtailed? Advertising comes to mind. What happens if your newspaper discovers a story which presents one of your biggest advertisers in a very bad light? What do you do if you know that by publishing the story an advertising contract will be terminated, resulting in tens of thousands of pounds in lost revenue, which in turn will lead to redundancies. Do you spike the story, knowing that another newspaper will publish it instead? Do you publish and be damned? Do you publish it but put the most positive spin possible on it?

We in the world of the religious media never have to worry about such dilemmas. More's the pity. We don't face such dilemmas because none of us receives such major advertising revenue that our newspapers or magazines could be compromised in this way. Were we to be faced with such a dilemma it would be a sign that our publications are in robust financial health.

But we do face problems of our own. The distribution network of some of our publications is quite different from that of the mainstream media. Some, perhaps most, religious publications are distributed by promoters, often members of the Legion of Mary, who sit at the back of the Church voluntarily, week in, week out, selling the paper. If it were not for their dedication, we would not even exist. However, there is a down side. In the world of the mainstream media, if a reader does not like a newspaper, he or she can stop buying it. The same applies to religious media. But if the reader who does not like a given story happens to be the promoter, then you are in danger of losing not one sale, but many, because the promoter may cancel his or her order on behalf of everyone. This has happened to *The Irish Catholic* on quite a number of occasions. There have also been times when the parish priest rather than the promoter has cancelled the order. It would not take too many cancellations of this sort to put a newspaper or magazine in very serious trouble indeed.

I can think of two ways in which a religious publication might find itself in this kind of situation. The first is where there is a complete change of editorial policy which adopts a full-speed-ahead and damn-the-torpedoes approach. If a publication decides to change its orientation completely, then it must be prepared to lose very many of its readers or even go out of business altogether.

When *The Tablet* took a stand against *Humanae vitae* its readership slumped, and it took the best part of a quarter of a century to recover it. How it survived financially in those years I do not know. If today it were suddenly to do another about-turn and support *Humanae vitae,* and support every decision of say, Cardinal Ratzinger, it would doubtless find itself in trouble again.

If a publication does decide to alter its editorial policy drastically, then care must be taken to ensure that most of those holding senior positions within the organisation support the change, i.e. owners, editors, chief reporters, etc. If any of these key personnel do not support the change, then they will likely resign or be forced to resign. No such change could even be contemplated, however, without the co-operation of the great majority of the key personnel. If the owner opposes the change, then forget it. It is not going to happen.

The second way a publication can get itself into trouble with its readers and/or promoters is where the editor unilaterally decides to change the publication's editorial direction. I have already dealt with this. More than likely the owner will step in.

This sort of thing takes place in both the religious and mainstream media. If it does not happen more often it is because owners and trustees ensure the editor is sympathetic to the paper's outlook before appointing him or her. What happens if a publication departs from its traditional territory? Think of the example of *Irish Press* newspapers. Once the dominant newspaper group on this island, it went into a decline from which it never recovered. Its readers abandoned it in droves. Why? While there is a variety of reasons I believe the main one is that the group lost direction. Apart from the Northern question (perhaps), it no longer knew where it stood on the great issues of the day. Finding de Valera's vision wanting in a changing Ireland, it was incapable of remaking his vision, and consequently the newspapers, for the Ireland of the 1990s. It didn't know where it stood. It didn't know whether it was a middle-brow or a low-brow venture. *The Irish Press* didn't know whether it was a tabloid or a broadsheet. It didn't know whether it was left-wing or right-wing, liberal or conservative.

Any institution which loses direction will go into decline. This is what happened to the Irish Press Group. It need not have happened. Take a newspaper such as *The London Times*. It has been in existence for over two hundred years. As the years have gone by it has evolved without ever losing its direction or identity. It is a broadly conservative paper which supports the Conservative party. Conservatism is caricatured as the politics of the past, and yet *The London Times* is as much a part of the newspaper scene today as it was two centuries ago.

We might ponder the question, why couldn't *The Irish Press* change while staying the same? I will leave this to others.

There is a point to these musings and it relates back to the question of press freedom. There is no such thing as absolute freedom when it comes to the press and editorial decisions. Even leaving aside interference from owners, advertisers, politicians, etc, an editor will be bound to some extent to the traditions of his or her paper. Abandon those traditions and your readers will likely abandon you.

Above all else the readers of a newspaper are the guardians of its traditions. It would be as unacceptable for the editor of *The Irish Times* to publish an anti-divorce editorial as it would for *The Irish Catholic* to publish a pro-abortion editorial. In both cases the readers, not to mention the staff and the owners and the trustees, would rebel. Protestations about editorial freedom would count for nothing.

I said earlier that press freedom is the product of a fairly complex matrix of forces. I hope I have gone some way towards demonstrating why this is so. Let me try to make it more clear by using the example of my own newspaper, *The Irish Catholic.*

The Irish Catholic is 109 years old. It was founded in 1888. It is privately owned. Today there are four directors and four shareholders. Three are Irish, one is Austrian. There are two misconceptions about *The Irish Catholic.* The first and more widespread one is that it is owned by the bishops. The second is that it is foreign-owned. Neither is true. The paper sells roughly 27,000 copies per week. Like most religious publications, that figure is considerably down on its glory days, but it is up by about 3,000 since the beginning of last year. In other words, its decline has been reversed.

As I have mentioned, it is sold mostly at the back of churches by promoters who are mostly members of the Legion of Mary.

The average reader is a fifty-five-year-old woman who is a devout Catholic, who goes to Mass at least once a week and worries about her children not going to Mass. She is generous almost to a fault in donating to charities – tens of thousands of pounds are channelled through our office each year – and she is loyal to the Pope.

The directors also, in effect, act as the trustees. One of the directors is a member of the family which founded the paper. This ensures that the paper maintains its long-standing traditions.

The editor must fit into this situation. The editor must be prepared to take over and lead a paper which has a particular view of the world, and he or she should broadly agree with that view. If not, then there will be conflict between the editor and the directors, promoters and readers.

Editorial freedom is not another word for absolute freedom. It is another word for freedom of the newspaper he or she edits. The editor should embody to a great extent his or her newspaper. Freedom of the press means freeing the newspaper to pursue whatever world view it represents free of outside interference.

In the case of *The Irish Catholic,* freedom means being free to take a line that is favourable to the Church, roughly aligned with the bishops, and orthodox. It could, I suppose, be said that this means the paper is not free because it simply follows and supports and tries to explain the teachings of the Church. This is only true if the stance is not freely chosen. In the case of *The Irish Catholic,* it is. One might as well say *The Guardian* in Britain is not free because it toes a roughly Labour party line, or that *The Daily Telegraph* is not free because it toes a roughly Conservative party line. So I say again, a newspaper is free if it is able to pursue its reason for being.

Why is freedom of the religious press important? Because it allows the religious press to carry out its function. This begs a further question: What is the function of the religious press? An obvious answer is to keep readers informed about the life of the Church. But this answer hides a deeper reason.

There are, I think, two possible justifications for its existence and they are not mutually incompatible. The first is to challenge the Church and its teachings. The second is to use the teachings of the Church to challenge society. As I say, these views are not incompatible, but one publication will lay more emphasis on one than the other.

Which is more important? Again, people will differ on this. We all agree that the Church is going through a very trying period at present. The scandals are in part to blame for this, but only in part. The Church was in decline anyway. On the Continent, in such places as France and Spain, Mass attendance is as low as three per cent in some places. This has been the case for several decades now, especially in France.

The reasons for this decline are beyond the remit of this talk, but clearly many people today feel the Church has nothing to say to them.

If you take the view that this is mostly the fault of the Church for not updating its teachings and practices, then you will logically take the view that the principal role of the religious press is to coax and prod and encourage the Church into doing so. At times, frustration with the slow, maybe non-existent pace of change, will turn to anger, and this anger will be directed at the authorities in the Church, specifically the bishops and the Pope.

On the other hand, if you take the view that the Church's message is as relevant as it ever was, and society is walking into a philosophical dead end, a spiritual wasteland (shades of T. S. Eliot here), then you will see it as the task of the Church to continue to preach its message to society in an effort to convince society of the truth of the Gospel as interpreted by the Church. Logically, if you take this view, then the primary task of the religious press will be to assist the Church in this endeavour.

Nothing is ever simple and there are at least two opposing views of everything. Here are two more. There are two other ways in which to judge whether the religious press is free or not. One says it is free if it can take a position substantially independent of that of the Church on a whole range of issues.

The other says it is free from the dominant view of society if it is counter-cultural. Nothing today is more counter-cultural than orthodox Christianity.

It is my own opinion that it is far more important today for the religious media to be counter-cultural. The Church is not the power it once was, thankfully. But new ideologies have rushed in to fill the vacuum – individualism, relativism, consumerism, statism, secularism, humanism – take your pick. The single biggest challenger to all of these systems is orthodox Christianity. Because of this, it is almost impossible today to find in the print or the broadcast media favourable analysis of say, John Paul II. It is as rare to find favourable treatment of some of the more unpopular Church teaching. It is much more common to find hostile stories about the Pope. It is much more common to find hostile stories about the teachings of the Church.

Let me deal with an especially controversial recent example, the paedophile scandals, the most appalling scandals to affect the Church since the Reformation. It is hard to know which aspect of these scandals was the worst, the fact that children were abused or the fact that the abuse was often covered up.

The media were duty-bound to report these scandals as they broke. This should not, however, blind us to the fact that there are different ways of treating a story.

A few months ago I sat in on a press conference at which former Equality and Law Reform Minister Mervyn Taylor announced plans for the Irish contribution to the European year against racism. At the conference the minister spoke about prejudice against Travellers. He highlighted the ways in which the media foster anti-Traveller attitudes. Asked to give examples, he referred to headlines such as 'Traveller charged with assault', or 'Traveller jailed for sex abuse'.

He wondered why it was necessary to include the word 'Traveller' in these headlines. By doing so the entire Traveller community was tarred with the same brush. It would be better, he suggested, if the headlines read, 'Man charged with assault', or 'Joe Bloggs jailed for sex abuse'.

Listening to him I was reminded of all those paedophile priest headlines. We never read headlines about paedophile farmers, or paedophile businessmen. It if is unacceptable to implicate all Travellers in the sins of a few, why is it more acceptable to implicate all priests in the sins of a few? It could be argued, I suppose, that quite unlike the Travelling community, the Church and its clergy were once placed on a pedestal. While this is a fair point and legitimates attacking the Church as an institution, it does not excuse placing all priests under a cloud of suspicion.

In addition, the reasons advanced for the incidence of paedophilia within the Church were extremely doubtful and yet were rarely challenged. For example, it was held that the rule of celibacy was partly responsible for some clerics abusing children. If men are barred from enjoying normal sexual relations, this line of argument went, then we can hardly be surprised when their sexual needs manifest themselves in appalling and perverse ways. Yet married men abuse their children and the incidence of child sexual abuse (to judge from American figures) is as high in Churches which do not have the rule of celibacy as it is in the Catholic Church.

In addition, even if the celibacy requirement were to be removed, there appears to be a general misunderstanding that it would not affect clerics such as Brendan Smyth, who is an Order priest.

The Catholic Church does stand indicted due to the paedophile scandals. However, because of the way the story was treated, the Catholic Church and its rule of celibacy became particularly associated with this blight. I also recall the treatment of the Bishop Roddy Wright story, when the Scottish bishop ran off with a divorcee last year. Again the rule of celibacy was to blame. If priests were allowed to marry, he would not have had to leave his post in order to live with her. Again, even a modicum of thought would reveal how absurd such a conclusion is. Married men are unfaithful to their wives, to their own marriage vows. If priests were allowed to marry, we would doubtless find priests also being unfaithful to their wives. A priest or a bishop abandoning his wife and children for another woman would be a cause of even worse scandal.

Again the impression given was that the Catholic Church had only itself to blame because of the unnatural requirement forced upon its clergy. This interpretation of clerical scandals was never properly challenged because our media are not sufficiently diverse. At the time of the Bishop Wright affair, several articles turned up in mainstream British papers defending the rule of celibacy. I did not encounter a single one in any Irish newspaper.

A vibrant religious press would have challenged this interpretation. A religious press which dissents from the dominant cultural norms is no substitute for a diverse mainstream media, but it would at least be a start. That is why I believe a truly free and useful religious press is one that is free from cultural captivity.

With the collapse of so many secular idols in this century, for example fascism, communism and socialism, and their replacement with ideologies that fail to satisfy, for example consumerism, this moment in which we live has been called 'the Catholic moment'. Catholicism provides the most coherent and philosophically defensible worldview, in the western world at least, today.

It is the task of the religious press in the late twentieth century to reflect that moment. A failure to do so is a failure indeed. It is more than that, it is a failure of nerve and imagination.

SAYING THE UNCOMFORTABLE THING

Kevin Hegarty

I like the fairy tale 'The Emperor's New Clothes'. You will recall it tells of a vain and foolish emperor duped by crooked tailors into parting with an enormous sum of money for a non-existent but supposedly exquisite gown. When he wore 'the gown' on parade in the capital city, the cheering crowds colluded in the deception, except for a young boy who had the temerity to blurt out that the emperor was naked.

All powerful institutions require for their purification someone to say uncomfortable things and ask awkward questions. The Catholic Church in Ireland cannot avoid this requirement. It has had a significant role in the shaping of Irish society and though now somewhat tattered, frayed and reduced in influence, it remains powerful. All powerful institutions regard the media with suspicion – there will always be a tension between the institution's desire to protect itself and the media's definition of the public right to know – but this suspicion is particularly acute in the Catholic Church in Ireland at the official level. One bishop has gone so far as to say that the media are responsible for 'a cancer of criticism and dissent, a cynicism about the faith'. A senior journalist, Michael O'Toole, the Dublin correspondent of *The Tablet,* claims that the loathing of some Irish priests and prelates for the media is palpable and has to be seen to be believed. I believe that this suspicion is unhealthy for the Church; for its internal workings and relationships and for its relationship with other institutions and experiences in Irish society.

Why is this suspicion so acute? It seems to me that the media are a product of the modern world and that this world in the main has been propelled by the insights of the Enlightenment and the French Revolution. Democracy has become the main form of government in civilised society. Freedom of speech has become an accepted and unquestioned value. Sceptre and crown have come tumbling down. Openness, transparency and accountability are the dominant emblems of the new age.

The Catholic Church has resisted the full implication of these generally positive insights. Vatican II was a valiant attempt to incorporate them, though this has been obscured by the restorationist imperative of Pope John Paul II's pontificate.

So I believe that the recent history of the Catholic Church in Ireland has left it in a poor position to appreciate the importance and value of a free press, both within and without the institution.

The nineteenth century was a creative period in Irish Catholic history. The Church responded substantially to the felt needs of the community in regard to education, health and social services, pre-dating the state's commitment to general welfare, and so contributed significantly to the modernisation of Irish society. At the leadership level, however, the latter half of the nineteenth century was a time of retrenchment. Cardinal Cullen, as leader of the Irish hierarchy from 1850 to 1878, imposed a monolithic uniformity on the episcopal conference at least in public; when he recommended a priest for appointment to the hierarchy his first question was inevitably a variant of Margaret Thatcher's later comment as to whether he was 'one of us'; gone now were the debates in local newspapers on appointments to bishoprics; gone too were the fascinating arguments in public between bishops, as happened most notably in the 1830s and 1840s over national and university education.

The new Irish state emerged through a consensus of Nationalism, Catholicism and middle-class economics. To many it seemed as if to be Irish meant to be Catholic. Partition ensured that the Church became even more influential. For the first time in centuries the Irish Catholic tradition found itself without a rival institution to come near matching its own force, so that it became the decisive factor in the self-image of the new state. In the circumstances it is perhaps not surprising that a semi-confessional state emerged where, in the somewhat jaundiced phrase of James Joyce, 'Christ and Caesar were hand in glove'. This confessionalism found expression in the enactment of laws in censorship and in the pronounced Catholic air of de Valera's 1937 Constitution. Despite the valiant and prodigious attempt of Mary Kenny to launder this history in her anguished paean of praise, 'Goodbye to Catholic Ireland', it was in the main an arrogant, oppressive and insular time and extremely suspicious and destructive of the value of individual experience. The novelist John McGahern telescoped the period well when he wrote:

> A kind of Utopia was created in the national psyche. It was as if suddenly the heavenly world and eternity had been placed on the twenty-six counties, administered by the Church and those who had done well out of independence.

In this atmosphere the Church received obsequious and uncritical coverage. Hagiography was seriously in vogue. I am reminded of Ambrose Bierce's definition of a saint as a 'dead sinner, revised and edited'. Church leaders were accustomed to the reverential treatment that used to be reserved for royalty before the tabloid mentality took hold. The comparison is, I think, apt. Bishops were a kind of Irish aristocracy. They lived in palaces and their consecrations were reported in the awed and sycophantic language used for the coronation of a monarch. In a drab Irish social landscape the colour purple added a cautious lustre to life. Their views were rarely questioned, their motives scarcely analysed. A flavour of the coverage is contained in *The Western People* newspaper in 1936 where it refers to Dr Naughton, the Bishop of Killala, in the following terms:

> Most Rev. Dr Naughton is the most beloved bishop who has ever had charged this ancient diocese. He has no interests save those of his master and flock. Approachable to all he holds a unique place in the affections of his flock. Still full of vigour mentally and physically, his flock pray that he will be long spared to carry on with dignity and success the duties of his high office.

All this and heaven too, you might say, and Dr Naughton merited this unrestrained and syrupy adulation merely because he had ordered that an extra Mass be said in the Cathedral every Sunday. It was a time when bishops and priests could send their sermons and pastoral letters to newspapers with the ultimatum that they be published in full or not at all. Awkward coverage could always be averted by a discreet word or phone call, the wink and elbow language of cosy complicity.

In one of his most celebrated poems, *'Annus Mirabilis',* Philip Larkin detected significant social change between the end of the Chatterly ban and The Beatles' first LP. It was also a time of change in Ireland, as the old order gave way and the consensus between Catholicism, Nationalism and middle-class economics began to disintegrate. The old Catholic solidarity has been destroyed by the liberalism, social mobility and the more pronounced democratic culture of recent decades. The long nineteenth century of Irish Catholicism has come to an end. A new class has emerged in Ireland – well educated, articulate and questioning, even sceptical of venerable institutions like the Church.

The Church's problems with the media – both within and without – arise, in the main, because it has failed to evolve a pastoral strategy and language that resonates with the contemporary experience of the new Ireland. Its leadership at episcopal and parish priest level is drawn from those whose formative experiences took place before Ireland changed. Many feel they are out of touch in an age of dialogue and diversity. They are travelling in a new world but using old maps.

I believe that at the leadership level the Church still hankers after a world where it is relatively unquestioned. I am afraid that this has been my experience. For three years I was editor of *Intercom,* a pastoral and liturgical journal published by the Catholic Communications Institute of Ireland under the aegis of the Communications Commission of the Episcopal Conference. I speak of this time with great reluctance. There was a public controversy about my removal from the position and such controversies have a way of typecasting a person. I had an interesting and worthwhile life before I edited *Intercom* and I have had an interesting and worthwhile life since. I had closed the book on that episode in my life quite some time ago but the subject of today's meeting and the importance of this week's conference has led me to open it for the last time. I believe it is a case study in the fear and suspicion that the Catholic Church leadership has of a free media.

I became editor of *Intercom* in 1991. I accepted the invitation to be editor because it seemed to me that Irish Catholicism needed a journal whose pages would be informed, dialogical, tolerant and inclusive – to do at the popular level what independent journals like *The Furrow, Doctrine and Life* and *Studies* do at the academic level. I was aware, however, that there were limitations on my objectives because of the journal's provenance. After all, a friend in the religious communication business had warned me that *Intercom*'s freedom was circumscribed. There were issues I could not raise, writers I could not employ because they would be too much out of kilter with the views of the Episcopal Conference. In retrospect, I can see I was imprisoned by an internal censorship.

Allowing for this, I still believed it was possible to open the pages of the journal to lively debate. I soon realised that my views made some bishops and priests uneasy. What I thought was a space for openness and diversity was described as a safe haven for dissidents and critics. Among the columnists I employed was Brendan Hoban, who often writes passionately and provocatively. In September 1993, in a piece on the need for greater lay involvement in the Church in Ireland, he wrote satirically that there were too many priests in Ireland and that their presence was impeding lay involvement. I soon realised that an appreciation of sub-Swiftian satire is not high among

Irish bishops and clergy. Among the frenzied complaints was one from a bishop, now deceased, who questioned my right to publish such an article. He was unwilling to respond in public as I asked him to do, but he wanted me to know that I had seriously transgressed. Soon afterwards I published a piece on the clerical sexual abuse of children. A northern bishop rang me about something else and in his convoluted way he got round to mentioning the article. He was surprised by its appearance. Did I not know that an episcopal committee was considering the issue? Was it not somewhat inopportune to place such an article in the magazine at this juncture? Perhaps he could mark my card in future? Another bishop queried raucously my editing of a rambling homily he had submitted, unsolicited, for publication. None of them wished to enter the debate and make their points in public. Behind these interventions lay a threatening penumbra, albeit veiled – they ultimately owned the magazine and I should be careful.

I must say I did not realise what true editorial freedom meant until recently when I was appointed editor of *Céide,* a new journal to be launched by President Mary Robinson on 23 August. The feeling of freedom is palpable. This journal will attempt to create a conversation and make connections between the arts and sciences, politics, economics and religion. It will be especially concerned to bring the marginalised into the conversation. I hope it will be a journal where different views will be aired, where positions will be argued forcefully but courteously, where there will be a robust respect for dissent, where those alienated from Church structures are given a voice and where no one is excluded because of a perceived unorthodoxy.

PART 5

THE CHURCH AND THE MEDIA IN NORTHERN IRELAND

THE NEED FOR DIALOGUE

Cardinal Cahal B. Daly

Although my brief is entirely to reflect on the responsibilities of Church and media in Northern Ireland, I understand that I am at liberty also to comment on wider questions of relations generally between Church and media.

If I may begin with a personal remark, I have to say, after thirty years as bishop, that the mainstream media have, on the whole, treated me generously and fairly, and I gladly and gratefully acknowledge that. From personal experience, I would conclude that, if one treats the media fairly and tries to be free of *a priori* complexes and suspicions, the media will reciprocate in kind.

I confess, however, that there are criticisms and suspicions about the media among ranks of the clergy at all levels. These cannot simply be dismissed as paranoia; there have been bishops and priests who themselves have been unfairly treated by the media, or whose close friends have been so treated, sometimes posthumously. Their hurt is understandable, their suspicion is justified. In any case, the almost universal and seemingly uncritical espousal by the media of what can fairly be called 'the liberal agenda' inevitably disposes the media to be critical of the Churches, but particularly and selectively of the Catholic Church. This is not a peculiarly Irish phenomenon. One American commentator, James Hitchcock, remarks:

Roman Catholics are the major minority group against whom it is still respectable to express prejudice and contempt.

Hitchcock was speaking of the Catholic Church in the United States of America. His words could be applied to some media in Ireland, though Roman Catholics in Ireland are not a 'minority group'. Hitchcock is a conservative Catholic, but this should not of itself disqualify his observation. Arthur Schlesinger Senior, who cannot be accused of *parti pris,* has remarked that a certain bias against the Catholic Church is 'the most deeply rooted of American prejudices'.

When I say that, on the whole, the mainstream media treated me generously and fairly, it remains true that a small number of columnists have directed at me remarks which were insulting and offensive, remarks which, I suggest, if they had been used about any leader of another Church or another faith, would have provoked outrage and protest, not least from other sections of the media. These, however, have been untypical and have usually emanated from idiosyncratic sources.

Positive contribution of the media

Let me say at the outset that my intention in this paper is not to be negative but to put forward for consideration some suggestions about ways in which the credibility of the media might be still further enhanced. For I regard it as highly important that the freedom of the media be respected and, indeed, be zealously guarded. The media worldwide and specifically in Ireland have provided a great service to society by conducting investigation into areas of suspected abuse of power or payments to politicians or into wrongs and injustices in society, into social evils such as poverty, unemployment, drugs and alcohol abuse, and domestic violence, which institutions in society might have preferred not to see publicly exposed. Several enlightened pieces of legislation have been in part due to exposure of the darker areas of our society.

The recent heightened concern throughout the world about such matters as child sex abuse and child pornography and about violence against women and other cruelty to children, owes something to the media's uncovering of evil, sordid and brutal activities which could otherwise have remained hidden. It is vitally important to society that the media have the freedom to investigate and explore and report matters in which accountability has been lacking and where reform is needed. The Church has benefited from responsible media probing of abuses and mature media questioning of Church activities. We in the Church should ourselves be active in making our institutions and our activities such as to have nothing to fear and nothing to hide from competent media enquiry. I am on record as stating that the media have done a service to the Church in Ireland in regard to scandals which have occurred. Though it could well be argued that the amount of space and time devoted to comment and speculation has been disproportionate, the media have discharged their rightful function in reporting these scandals. An essential response to scandals is to establish effective procedures aimed at preventing their recurrence. In regard to the horror of child sexual abuse, for example, the Catholic Church authorities in Ireland now have in place clear and public guidelines for dealing with complaints made against priests or religious.

'Tabloidisation' of the media

Few, I think, would deny that there has been a slippage of standards in the media over recent years. The frantic rush, in some sectors of the media, for the 'scoop' and the 'exclusive', the frenetic competition for readership and listenership or viewership, have led to such abuses as increasing violation of embargoes, a greater frequency in the passing off of sheer speculation as information from the ubiquitous but anonymous and forever untraceable 'sources'. Today's speculation may prove tomorrow to be yesterday's fable, but some newspapers seem to rely on people's short memories, content to let today's headlines sell today's papers, and let tomorrow look after itself!

Still more serious is the blurring of the distinction once regarded by the media as sacrosanct, between 'facts' and 'comment', or between reporting and advocacy. Sometimes reporters of public debate themselves become participants on one side of the debate. It is surely disturbing when, over a whole series of referendum debates, most of the national media, whether in editorial articles or comment and feature columns, are united on one side of a debate on which the electorate are deeply, and, in the case of the recent divorce referendum, almost evenly, divided. Are there not serious questions to be asked here? Do the media see their role as being to report democratic debate in society fairly, or to influence debate in one direction solely? There is surely matter here for serious reflection and discussion.

A study of the language used by the media over the duration of these debates would be very interesting. I believe that such a study would show that the terms used to describe, for example, pro-life and anti-divorce protagonists are invariably pejorative terms, and those used to describe proponents of abortion or divorce are invariably favourable and, indeed, commendatory. I suggest that here also is an area requiring honest self-examination on the part of people working in media.

Furthermore, the emphasis in modern media seems to be moving towards entertainment rather than information; or, perhaps more accurately, towards something in between, something which has been called 'infotainment'. Hence the emergence of a new phenomenon which Norman Mailer has called the 'factoid', something which is not factually true made into a 'fact'. In short, there seems to be a kind of creeping 'tabloidisation' of the mainstream media, and this must be a source of concern to many people within the media themselves, as well as to the public.

The media are, of their nature, voracious creatures with insatiable appetites. They have large slots of time and wide acres of print to fill, day by day, whether or not there is real 'news' available to fill them. Through a variety of panel discussions, chat shows, access radio or television shows, health and 'agony aunt' columns, etc, the media have come to take on something of the roles of a police complaints service, indeed a criminal investigation role, a customer complaints service, a health service monitor, a universal ombudsman, a counselling service, even concerning moral and spiritual matters, etc. In diverse areas such as these, much care has been taken by professional organisations and others over the decades or the centuries to put in place well-trained professionals and well-tested codes of practice and rules and safeguards, all in the interests of justice and fairness for those affected. In the judicial system, for example, there are rules of evidence, standards of proof, a presumption of innocence until guilt is proven, a placing of the onus on the accuser to prove guilt rather than on the accused to prove innocence. Thus a corpus of judicial process has been gradually built up over the centuries, which, while it does not guarantee justice, at least provides conditions in which just verdicts are more likely than unjust ones. I submit that hitherto very little thought seems to have been given by the media to developing similar ethical and moral standards to govern their own activities in comparable fields of complaint, accusation, rumours and suspicion.

A code of ethics for the media
I mention all this simply to point to what I suggest is a need for a more formal code of ethics for journalists and media personnel. I believe that media freedom is essential for a free society and is a prerequisite for the healthy functioning of democracy. I believe that political control or political manipulation of the media is an abomination. I believe likewise that commercial control of the media needs constant scrutiny and that media monopolies are a danger in a democratic society.

Harman Grisewood said, 'every broadcast is a moral act'. So is every editorial or news story or feature or article. All the more necessary, therefore, it seems to me, is voluntary agreement by media themselves on the adoption of an ethical code of journalistic and media practice. In an ideal world, this would be sufficient to prevent abuses. In the real world, something more is needed in the form of some kind of media ethics and standards council, whose findings would be given a degree of binding force. There is also need for formal training for media principals and practitioners in the moral issues which arise in electronic and print media.

Furthermore, I believe that there has not been in this

country nearly enough analysis and criticism and self-criticism of media by media. Judgement of one's peers is usually the most effective, as well as generally the fairest form of judgement. At present, it would seem that every institution in Ireland is subject to judgement by the media, except the media themselves.

One journalist, at least, has had the courage to sound a critical and a warning note. I wish to quote from something which Andy Pollak wrote in 1995.

> I hold no brief for Catholic bishops. However, as a journalist, what I do hold precious are the values of honesty, fairness and balance in reporting all things, plus sensitivity and a keen awareness of what is in the public interest when writing about people's private lives. And that includes priests' and bishops' lives.
>
> I would only ask my colleagues to be extremely wary of the example set by the English tabloid press, who would have our news values dictated by the 'lowest common denominator', popular appetites which unscrupulous newspaper bosses and editors have helped to create in the first place. I have seen some alarming signs ... that journalistic standards in this country are slipping in that direction.
>
> *The Irish Times,* 3 October 1995

The media in Northern Ireland

The media in Northern Ireland, over nearly twenty-seven years of conflict, seem to me, on the whole, to have acted with integrity. Journalists and photographers have often displayed great courage in the course of duty in the face of personal danger. The media have been accused of concentrating on atrocities rather than on analysis and background; this criticism seems to me to apply more to the British and foreign media than to the Irish-based media, whether North or South. Some media have, on occasion, let themselves be manipulated by paramilitary organisations for their own propaganda purposes, such as pre-arranged print- and photo-reportage of training exercises, illegal road blocks, etc. This has been relatively rare, but it has been reprehensible.

Sometimes media have tended also to give exaggerated emphasis to polarisation of views, to the comparative neglect of moderate voices, although moderates are in the majority in both communities. It is often spokespersons for the extremist elements or parties, or from the more extreme representatives of the mainstream parties, who are called upon to comment on events or on statements or to participate in panel discussions. The no-saying decibels of the one side and the clapped-out clichés of the other, tend to evoke a tired derision rather than carry conviction. Nevertheless, in a society desperately in need of moderate leadership, less media emphasis on polemical and adversarial styles of debate would be helpful. In the early days of the radio, someone optimistically described it as 'the nation in dialogue with itself'. In a community of two divided political communities, some would say two nations, the media are the best opportunity for each 'nation' to listen to and try to understand the other. Disputatious and controversial spokepersons, who try to shout down rather than listen to one another, are positively unhelpful. Many people feel the media give such people too much exposure, and that thereby the media may serve to increase polarisation rather than promote mutual understanding.

The broadcasting media

There has obviously been partisanship on the part of some media. The perception of both the BBC and UTV in both Nationalist and Unionist areas has often been negative. Coming from an avowedly pro-establishment, and therefore pro-British and pro-Unionist background in the pre-Troubles period, both organisations had much leeway to make up, particularly so far as the Nationalist and Catholic community was concerned. Both BBC and UTV were considered by the Unionist and Loyalist community in the past as being by nature and of right 'their' broadcasting organisations, so that efforts to reflect the two political and religious traditions more equally were doomed to be judged by some to be biased in favour of Nationalists.

It must be admitted, however, that a dilemma faces all media in Northern Ireland, namely that what is perceived as impartiality on one side is judged partisan on the other; indeed, objective and fair reporting is likely to be judged partisan by elements in both communities. In Northern Ireland, perceptions have more impact than reality; indeed, for many people, perceptions replace reality. For broadcasting organisations to be perceived on both sides as truly non-partisan sources on news and comment, requires a task for which Sisyphus himself might understandably have been unwilling to make a career change!

The print media

The local print media in Northern Ireland have equally come out of a politically partisan past. The Unionist *Newsletter* accomplished the extraordinary feat of finding different words over nearly twelve months in what seemed like every second editorial to attack that 'infamous diktat', the Anglo-Irish

Agreement! All the more remarkable and praiseworthy, therefore, are the steps which this newspaper has taken towards more objective and less partisan reporting and comment. History was made, in Northern Ireland terms, when the *Newsletter* called for a new investigation of the events of Bloody Sunday in Derry, and again when the *Newsletter* and the Nationalist *Irish News* issued a joint editorial, calling for compromise in order to avert the disaster of another Drumcree in 1997.

The Belfast Telegraph, for its part, following and further developing the enlightened policy of a truly great editor, John Sayers, has succeeded in achieving a balanced cross-community readership and a balance of reporting and comment and features which in Northern Ireland terms is admirable.

The Irish News has undergone a significant transformation over recent years. While retaining its Nationalist ethos, this newspaper, under its recent editors, has genuinely sought to reflect Unionist views fairly, to have a balanced spread of contributors to features columns, to adhere to a moderate editorial policy and offer fair and balanced political analysis. A real service to peace and reconciliation in this troubled community is provided by newspapers which purposefully set out to help one community to understand the other and overcome inherited preconceptions about the other.

Among national newspapers and radio and television organisations in the Republic, which, of course, also have a circulation and listenership and viewership in Northern Ireland, reportage and comment about Northern Ireland has, on the whole, striven to be fair and balanced. It is perhaps natural that they tend to lean toward the Nationalist viewpoint, while trying to be fair to the Unionist outlook. It would undoubtedly contribute still further to greater mutual understanding if these media outlets gave more space and voice to Unionist spokespersons, reflecting the various trends within Unionism, and avoiding the imbalance which can be projected by people of more extreme views, who often seem to receive disproportionate space and time in all media.

Honesty commands me to express concern about a perceptible trend in certain newspapers, where some columnists have taken considerable time and trouble to direct their undoubted talent into condemnation, or at least dismissal of the Northern peace process and, most regrettably, into sustained criticism of its chief architect, John Hume. Their zeal in condemning the IRA is commendable. But surely those people within the Republican movement who seem to be trying to bring the movement away from physical force and into peaceful democratic politics deserve encouragement, not rejection; and surely John Hume, who more than anyone else in Ireland has laboured for peace, to the neglect of his health and at real personal and political risk, deserves credit and support, not condemnation. The peace process might fail; but it will always have been the more noble thing to have tried to bring peace and to have failed than not to have tried. If the peace process were finally to fail, which, may God avert, I hope we will be spared anyone's 'I told you so'.

Reporting of news from the Republic

A welcome development in the media of Unionist background is the tendency to report events and opinions in the Republic more positively and to analyse Irish Government policies in respect of Northern Ireland more objectively than was until quite recently the case. There seems to be less of an inclination among some Unionist spokespersons nowadays to treat the Republic as a 'hostile foreign state', or a 'Roman Catholic Church-run' or 'priest-ridden' society, or as a backward 'banana republic' than was formerly the case.

Both in terms of non-partisan reporting and analysis within Northern Ireland, and in terms of fair reporting and comment regarding the Republic of Ireland, some British tabloids circulating in Northern Ireland compare very unfavourably with locally based media. It is time that some of the 'non-quality' British media operating and broadcasting into Northern Ireland and into the Republic came to terms with the new sets of relationships which are now formally accepted as official policy aims by both the British and Irish Governments and by the majority of people in the two islands.

To conclude my remarks about media in respect of Northern Ireland, I judge that, in this deeply divided society, Irish media, both Northern and Southern, have, overall, had a positive rather than a negative effect. They have covered conflict at its most brutal with courage. They have reported words and acts of forgiveness and efforts for reconciliation and peace fully and often memorably. They have reported political developments with increasing objectivity. They have tried in varying degrees to erect bridges of communication across the divides. They are tentatively helping us to image a different and transformed kind of Northern Ireland, a different kind of island of Ireland, than we have known; and imagining difference and transformation can be an important step towards bringing about transforming change.

Need for Church-media dialogue
Might I be allowed, by way of conclusion to both sections of this paper, to quote something I said in March 1996:

There has been a perception, moreover, that, in some sections of the media, something of a campaign against the Catholic Church has been carried on. I believe that editors, producers and journalists generally should honestly address this perception and should ask to what extent this may be true, and to what extent the ethics of journalism, requiring balance, fairness and integrity, may have been transgressed. I do not think that any newspaper in Ireland would want to see itself perceived as 'anti-Catholic'. But perhaps the time has come for some soul-searching by journalists and editors and media commentators in this regard.

There must, however, be corresponding soul-searching by us Church people about our attitudes to the media. Too often our attitudes are defensive and suspicious. We could make the media hostile towards us by first assuming that they are hostile. It is strange that we, who talk so much about the need for dialogue and trust in the North, seem to be ourselves so wary of dialogue with media people and so lacking in trust of journalists. It is not that we as Church people should expect the media to 'do us favours'. Church and media have different responsibilities and we must each respect the other in our respective fulfilment of those responsibilities. However, trust between people evokes trust, while mistrust spawns answering mistrust. Dialogue is, after all, the Church's business. As Pope Paul VI said thirty years ago, we must be constantly striving to put the Church's message 'into the mainstream of human discourse'. Dialogue with media is an indispensable part of the task.

There is, of course, a sense in which media, operating within a 'liberal consensus' culture in our Western world will, almost necessarily, be at variance with the teaching of the Catholic Church. Catholic Church teaching is, almost of necessity, counter-cultural in terms of many of the core values of modern Western liberal culture. It is in this sense that Cardinal Newman remarked that, when the Church ceases to be criticised by the world, it is because she is no longer proclaiming the truth revealed by Jesus Christ. We must not, however, develop a 'victim complex'. We must embrace what is good in modern culture, confident that all that is true and noble and good derives ultimately from Christ, who enlightens every man and woman coming into this world.

PART 6

THE WAY FORWARD

LEARNING FROM EACH OTHER

Oliver Maloney

I would like to take up some issues raised which seem to me to be particularly significant and also to introduce one or two new topics. The purpose of this week's gathering was to achieve some meaningful dialogue between media and Church. It has done so successfully. One of the fruits of authentic dialogue is that it opens up the possibility to those involved that there may be blemishes and deficiencies in their own outlook – previously unacknowledged elements of prejudice, ignorance, suspicion or hostility. If real progress in relationship is to be made it is not sufficient simply to identify and then discard this inhibiting baggage; we need to examine it carefully, establish its provenance, and then strive imaginatively to forge fresh links based on newly found mutual respect. This is what we have been doing this week. We might comfort ourselves that the process we have been engaged in itself represents an advance, even if the outcome is unclear and the future difficult to discern.

The dynamics of the media/Church relationship

This week's conference represents a beginning, but no more than that. The building of relationships based on trust and integrity is a fragile undertaking which takes much time and is susceptible to setbacks and misunderstandings. Above all it entails a genuine attempt to come to grips with the dynamics within which the other party operates. One of the difficulties which our exchanges identified in the relationship between Church and media was an inherent difference in dynamics. Media concern with elements of competitiveness, profit, simplification, personalities, openness and urgency are given no great weight by many in the Church; on the other hand, Church preoccupation with tradition, continuity, fidelity and authority seems remote and strange to many media people. These misunderstandings lead to gross stereotyping, of the bishop-bashing/media-bashing variety.

These differences in dynamics are important and colour the relationship in some respect. But I am not sure that I agree with Bishop Flynn when he derives from these differences an antithetical model in which the Church is seen as concerned with reconciliation, the eternal and the profound, as opposed to the media who are presented as inherently conflictual, ephemeral and superficial. This type of analysis has also been put forward by the American Jesuit theologian, Avery Dulles.

The difficulty about this approach is that in substantial measure it is merely rhetorical. Can we really deny large elements of the conflictual, the ephemeral and the superficial in our own outlook, having regard to the history of the Church on this island? And did not, for example, the unforgettable television pictures of the late Senator Gordon Wilson cradling the body of his dying daughter in his arms and forgiving her killers constitute a most powerful expression of that enduring faith and forgiveness which is at the heart of the Christian vision?

So the reality is more complex than it appears. During the week one contributor from the floor made the important point that media people do not recognise as valid the image of media presented by the Church; and Church people do not recognise as valid the image of Church presented by the media. In a sense both sides are failing to address the reality as distinct from the perception of the other's position. The reality is in part mundane: it is one of most Church people seeking genuinely to build community and of most journalists striving genuinely to observe the ethic of fairness, balance and integrity in their work. Why then the mutual suspicion? I suspect it arises less from news reporting or news analysis or specialist work on religious issues and more from perceived imbalance or prejudice in opinion columns in the press and chat shows on radio and television. These are frequently seen as trivialising serious issues or as being partial and unfair.

Journalists tend to be an opinionated breed, none more so than those who write columns of comment or host chat shows. Frequently it is this very trait which is the reason for their being given these jobs in the first place. Some chat show hosts and newspaper columnists undeniably are partial, prejudiced, lazy or incompetent. Of course, the same can be said of some Church people! Such is life. The difference is that media people have privileged access to air time or column space which the ordinary citizen does not enjoy; their views, interests, likes and dislikes get a constant airing. Their primary orientation is to engender interest among the audience or readers, irrespective of the topic. They may, therefore, take liberties which experts might frown on, or explore unorthodox perspectives. That is the nature of a free press.

What do Church people do, therefore, when they feel that their concerns are being dealt with unfairly on chat shows and in opinion columns? The answer is that for the most part they do nothing. There may be a professional response from a Church press officer, but their lines of communication are usually with religious affairs correspondents who are not the people who are deemed to have offended. I can say that I received very few representations in this area during my time in RTÉ, and unfortunately the bulk of these were of a trivial nature.

What should Church people do? My advice may seem trite, but it has a basis in experience: it is that you have to protest. Protest is so often the vehicle of change. It is ineffective when it takes the form of a scatter-gun attack, but will be treated seriously by most organs of the media if it is measured and specific. Media people, no more than others, take seriously serious criticism of their work, and such criticism can frequently be the first step in meaningful dialogue on real live issues of difference.

Church as institution

A relevant question which the Church might address is why do some Church activities (e.g. the social analysis of CORI, or drug rehabilitation projects) receive significant and generally favourable media coverage, while other aspects of the Church do not. I believe the reason is that so many of these other activities are seen by media as being institutional in character (they are dimensions of the other face of the Church, to use Helena O'Donoghue's phrase) and are therefore evaluated by the media by reference to the same criteria as other institutions.

I find it difficult to quarrel with this media judgement because the operating model of Church in this state is still centred on the institution, the preservation of doctrinal orthodoxy, and the maintenance of ecclesiastical structures and influence. The central focus of the institution is on facilitating the passing on intact of revealed truths to the next generation, principally by making secure the apparatus currently available for that purpose.

That is a reasonable focus in so far as it goes; but perhaps it does not go far enough. To illustrate why, I want to make a number of theological points. Many of us were reared with a notion of Christian faith as being concerned primarily with the next world and essentially as involving assent to a corpus of beliefs which were taught dogmatically by the Church. But faith in God is more than this. Pre-eminently, it is faith rooted in a particular history, a history which culminates in Jesus Christ. And the primary movement in the Church is the freedom of the Holy Spirit to interpret the Christ-event to each generation. Church teachings and dogmas are an attempt to formulate the experience of the Christ-event and of the movement of the Spirit in the historical life of the Church. So these dogmas and teachings are thoroughly historical, and though they are true they share the properties of other human formulations in that they are limited by perspective, language and culture. They tell the truth but they don't exhaust it.

Because the Spirit speaks to each new generation, there is a responsibility on Church leaders to listen attentively to the faith experiences of their flock; to be open to the signs of the Spirit operating among the body of the faithful. This involves concerning themselves not just with the ontological coherence of expressions of faith, but more urgently with the lived experience of faith in the daily struggles of life and death in our communities. There is involved here an emphasis on Christian faith as practical rather than conceptual, and as not being primarily about a body of truths but of following the example of Jesus Christ and creating redeemed communities. This is precisely what many Church groups are doing and it is this aspect of the Church's work that is acknowledged and finds a positive response in even the most secular of media.

Perhaps this might raise questions for Church leaders as to where they should be channelling and seen to be channelling their energies, and as to the primary focus of their ministry. Is that focus on matters of administration, finance, organisation, protocol, membership of Roman congregations, and the issuing of pastoral letters and directives? Or is it on being with their people as a reassuring presence to help them to experience the living Christ in a largely unbelieving world amidst the many challenges and vicissitudes of life? If as Church we place, and are seen to place, the primary emphasis on institutional factors – and I am not suggesting an either/or situation – we should not be surprised if the media judge us in that light. We cannot escape the fact that the combination of democratic imperatives, and the growing sense of freedom of Irish people, has altered irreversibly the context in which the community of faith operates and in which its witness is judged.

Media, Church and pluralism
During the week one senior media person spoke in approving terms of a pluralist society. This has been a central preoccupation of many media who have avidly documented the perceived movement of Irish society in that direction. Enthusiasm is, however, no substitute for perspicacity. The Irish state has in fact been a pluralist society in many respects for some considerable time. Indeed, if there is a significant deficit in pluralism in the state, it is in the media themselves, where the Independent Group has an unhealthy dominance, which regulators urgently need to address.

What is perceived by media as pluralism is all too frequently secularism: secularism is the negation of pluralism. Those who advocate a wholly secular approach to the organisation of our civic life show an intolerance of the legitimacy of views other than their own. There is an impression in religious circles that the Dublin media is dominated by liberals. In one sense I wish it were true! Because the reality seems to me to be that there is in fact a paucity of media liberals in the classic sense of the term liberal – people who demonstrate a tolerance of views other than their own, and who are dedicated to upholding core values in society in the interest of the common good. A form of non-pluralist orthodoxy prevails in some media circles that you have to be feeble-minded or dumb to be religious.

Instead of media liberals, we have what the British Chief Rabbi has recently called libertarians, advocates of the notion that morality is not a public but a purely private concern. The main plank in this outlook is the proposition that moral imperatives should be reduced to a single consideration – that one may not act in a way that is harmful to others.

This particular moral vision characterises much thinking on moral issues in the media and increasingly in the wider society. It is attractive to Christians who perhaps don't think deeply about these matters, and is one of the reasons why the Christian perspective on moral issues has difficulty in being heard in contemporary debate. I suggest it is a minimalist view of what human life in society is all about. The Christian view is that life is a blessing and freedom is God's gift, and that they should be used to enable us to grow as people through loving our neighbour, including our enemy. There is a world of difference between not acting in a way that is harmful to others and loving your enemy. The Christian view accepts, of course, that the other should not be harmed, but argues that the moral vision cannot stop at that; there is much more. There is much more basically and essentially because of a belief in Jesus Christ – in his teaching, his life, and ultimately his vindication by God in the resurrection. Christians have experienced this as a better way. Their authority for their moral views includes the authority of lived experience. The challenge to Christians is to show others not just by what we say, but by the way we live as Church, that the genuine Christian moral attitude is more complete, more compassionate, and ultimately more human.

If we accept the prevailing fashion that morality is a purely private and personal matter, how is it possible to build community based on the acceptance of moral norms? The bishops of England and Wales have identified this dilemma in a recent document on the common good. They stress that some idea of the common good, common to believers, agnostics and atheists, and respectful of our various cultures, is essential for the functioning of a plural society. I suggest that there is an opportunity, if not a compelling need, for both Church and media to promote wider public discourse on what might constitute an idea of the common good for the Ireland of the twenty-first century.

The media debate on rights
A related issue is the public debate on rights, and in recent years media and Church have found themselves in opposite camps on issues of rights, most notably in the public clash between the supporters of the right to life and supporters of what is termed the right to choose. This debate has frequently been lacking in nuance. Nuance in these matters cannot be dismissed as some kind of academic pedantry because the

principles involved have far-reaching consequences. There is a real danger of inflating the language of rights, and I am not convinced that either Church or media have recognised the danger such inflation poses for the cohesion of our society. A right is a necessary claim on something, and not everything asserted to be a right is one. The advocacy of rights has to be balanced by an equivalent emphasis on duties and must always by tempered by regard for the common good, to which all have an obligation to contribute. Both Church and media may need to reflect on the extent to which their contributions in this area have been a help or a hindrance to genuine public understanding.

Media and dissent within the Church

Media treatment of dissent within the Church is resented. The perception is that media delight in creating divisions and give favoured treatment to those who challenge authority. The issue is not unlike the wider issue of media coverage of minority views in society as a whole. Important institutions within society must be open to questioning and exploration in the public interest, and media people must be free to engage responsibly in such questioning and to give appropriate coverage to minority views and to dissent. While the handling of such coverage may be criticised, the principle itself is not in my view open to challenge. As a general rule the volume of media coverage given to dissenting or minority views ideally should reflect the volume of support which those views attract in the wider society (particularly where public service broadcasting is concerned). There is an appropriate proportionality. However, the absence of such support does not automatically mean that media coverage of such views should be avoided.

Given these considerations I think that Church objections to media coverage of dissent or criticism within its ranks is not in principle justifiable. Indeed, there may be an element of shortsightedness involved. I say this because the original Christians were people of protest – the dissenters of their own time. They rejected the view that they should conform within mainstream Judaism and the essence of their stand was an assertion of conscience. The day may soon come when Christians will find themselves in a minority in a society which less and less accepts the normality of religious commitment. If that day comes it is those who now consider themselves orthodox who will be claiming from the media the right of dissent, the right to be heard.

Consumerism: enemy of media and Church
I want to end with what I regard as the common enemy of Church and media – consumerism. Consumerism has always been resisted in the Church's social teachings. But Irish media for the most part are commercial enterprises, so that the commercial ethic necessarily forms part of their outlook. Nowadays, marketing strategies seem to outrank journalistic considerations in the determination of general media policy. The tension between those two elements has been a long-standing feature of the media landscape, and the balance has now, in my view, swung too far in one direction. The excesses of the tabloid press have their roots in a particularly strong attachment to the commercial ethic. Respect for basic human dignity largely takes second place in the race to sell more papers and make more profits. While vulgarity, prurience and bad taste are not necessarily to be welcomed, there is an objectionable pattern of journalism emerging which involves the sneering repudiation of many of the values which make

community-building possible. This should not simply be passed off with a shrug of the shoulders and an excuse of powerlessness.

I want to pose one question in this regard to both Church and media. Where are the prophets who will challenge the Murdoch-like personalities who fund and control, and ultimately benefit financially from these monuments to unrestrained free-market ideology? Are these personalities the new untouchables?

The way ahead

At the end of the day, Church and media have things to learn from each other: the Spirit of God is not to be found exclusively in either. The media speak in a language accessible to ordinary people, and I agree with the director-general of RTÉ, Bob Collins, that Church matters are not, as is commonly suggested, uniquely complex and uniquely incapable of being dealt with adequately in the course of normal media treatment. The respect which the Church seeks to give to all is an approach which media might value more. Both have important things to say to society and state, and to each other. On close examination, the visions of society which responsible Church people and journalists favour would not, I suggest, be all that far apart; the core values of the Judaeo-Christian tradition are admired by most Irish journalists. None the less, it would be naïve to postulate a relationship between them which is free from conflict and tension. I find it useful to remember that harmony refers to a state in which tensions are maintained in balance; it does not mean the absence of tension. That seems to me to be a realistic aspiration for the relationship between media and Church in the years ahead.

THE WORD THAT GOES FORTH

Eamonn Conway

Introduction

The purpose of the summer school on media and the Churches was educational. It was meant to be an opportunity for broadcasters, journalists, Church spokespersons and the general public to come to a better understanding of how media report Church news and of what the Church has to do in order to proclaim its message more effectively.

The initiative for the conference was taken by a Church body. It is therefore appropriate that we conclude the publication of these papers with a reflection on the responsibilities of the Church in a world in which media play a critical role.

What no eye has seen, nor ear heard

That which 'no eye has seen, nor ear heard, nor the human heart conceived',[1] is revealed in and to the Christian community. Viewed from the perspective of the community's faith, we have a gifted insight into the dignity of all creation. We have an 'exclusive', an 'inside' story to tell. God's most complete and graphic rendition of God's own story lives on in us as a community. In the story of Jesus, God 'tells all'. Times past, there was an economy with the facts, partial glimpses, hints of where the truth might lie, games of hide-and-seek. When Moses, for example, interviews God about his future plans for the chosen race he doesn't know what to make of the deliberately evasive answer, 'I am who I am', and scholars are unsure to this day just how to translate it.[2] With Jesus, however, God holds nothing back: 'In him we see our God made visible, and so are caught up in love of the God we cannot see.'[3] In Jesus two stories, God's and ours, become one. God's story is the beginning and end of ours, and as the plenitude of God is made known to us, human dignity and depth is also unfolded before us.

What is disclosed is not marked for our eyes only. The Good News is for all, and for this very reason must be proclaimed. It must be proclaimed so that by hearing it, all people may grow in hope and in love.[4] Right at the heart of our celebration of the Eucharist we proclaim bread broken and shared and a cup poured out, *for all,* in Jesus' memory. To reach all people with this insight, and primarily for this reason, the Church must relate to the media fully, wisely and responsibly.

Differing anthropologies

But there is a problem. As institutions, media and Church march to different drums. This becomes quite apparent when one reflects, for example, on the treatment of people who have, by any standard, committed acts which can only be considered reckless, corrupt, perverted or depraved. The media, perhaps reflecting the personal stances of many readers and viewers, pass ready judgement on people's lives. Words like 'disgraced' or 'shamed' or 'crooked' almost replace people's Christian names. The message is: these people are beyond redemption.

The Church, on the other hand, if it is faithful to its mission, reserves judgement. And this is why, for example, priests and religious can and must stand beside the graves of people who may have done outrageous things, even if to some this is a source of hurt or of scandal. Newspapers and television intersect with people's lives only for a few brief moments to record events of great triumph or disaster. But the Church does not settle for the edited highlights. It stays with a person's life story, stretching it, expanding it with the story of the Gospel.[5] The Christian community moves easily from the lonely, craggy hilltop of Calvary, with its stench of betrayal and decay, to that place where, even while still dark, joy fills the emptiness of the tomb. Words of compassion, of forgiveness, of promise and hope are not difficult to find for those who are living and dying with the Lord.[6] There is nothing in human experience which is not only accounted for, but interpreted beyond words in the story of Jesus of Nazareth. And so in the face of apparent no-win situations the Church holds before all people the possibility of forgiveness and the power of love. Whatever its reputation for preaching the loss of heaven and the pains of hell, the Church has always taught that the final chapter in someone's life is never written until they die, and even in death it remains hidden from us. All we know with certainty is that because God is co-author of our lives, no one is beyond redemption or conversion. The rest is a mystery; disturbing at times, but still a mystery.

Truth and freedom

The essential difference between media and Church becomes clear when we examine two concepts fundamental to both institutions: truth and freedom. It is the responsibility of newspapers and television to tell the truth, 'to tell it as it is'. Truth is generally understood as information or facts which, it is perceived, the public has a right to know. Thus, the truth is 'revealed' and people or institutions are 'exposed'.

The truth of a person or a situation, according to Christian anthropology, is not reducible to information or facts, however accurate. When we look at the Gospels we see that truth is an encounter and an invitation to conversion. Jesus confronted people with the truth of his ministry every day. We need only recall the stories of Zacchaeus, the ostracised tax-collector; the Samaritan woman at the well who had five husbands and no husband; or Jesus' encounter with Pilate, who was determined to maintain the *Pax Romana* at any cost.[7] Encounters with the truth were sometimes painful. But when people were 'exposed', it was not just to their wrongdoing, but also to their dignity and worth before God. People were not left condemned and helpless by the revelation of their falsity. Their exposure was in the very same moment an experience of love and an invitation to conversion. People saw themselves as God saw them. This opened up possibilities and choices. Not everyone accepted the truth: Zacchaeus did, and he was liberated from his greed; the woman at the well went away with more questions than answers; Pilate washed his hands. Those who accepted the truth were freed, those who rejected it were condemned. They were not condemned by Jesus, who still loved them, perhaps loved them even more. They were condemned by themselves because now they knew who they were before God and, refusing to accept it, were living a contradiction.

'The truth will make you free', we read in John's Gospel.[8] Contrary to the word on the street, the Church is very much in favour of freedom. But by freedom the Christian community does not mean the absence of any restriction, the freedom to do one thing today and something else tomorrow. This is not human freedom and does not bring genuine happiness or fulfilment. Human freedom, as the

Church understands it, is the capacity to fulfil our potential as human beings. When Jesus spoke of freedom it was usually in the context of freedom from sin or disease.[9] Both sin and disease prevent people from living fully human lives. Sin is deliberately missing the mark in terms of living in a wholly human way. Our lives have potential and each of our free decisions is a step towards or away from achieving it. We are free when we take decisions which advance us along the path towards fulfilment. Contrary decisions enslave us and draw our whole lives into contradiction.

In a society which is pluralist and liberal, there will be conflicting notions of truth and freedom. And in a democratic society all opinions carry equal rights. The media, if they are to be fair and balanced, must treat each opinion with the same respect. Christianity, however, does not see its understanding of truth and freedom as simply one among others. It believes that in Jesus Christ, truth and freedom find an absolute reference point in human history, and one which is accessed in the Christian community. This places Christianity on a collision course with those who see truth and freedom merely in relative terms, as matters of public opinion which can vary according to circumstance, time and place. It is important, then, for both Church and media authorities to be realistic about the extent to which media at the service of a pluralist and liberal society can respect the Christian community's understanding of truth and freedom.

Does this mean that people who do not believe in Jesus Christ cannot be at the service of truth and freedom? Earlier in these papers, the editor of *The Sunday Tribune,* Matt Cooper, quoted Archbishop Desmond Connell as saying that:

it is not surprising that there should be a close correspondence between the law of the land and Catholic moral teaching in respect of a host of crimes from tax evasion to rape. Such crimes are forbidden by the law, not because Catholic teaching rejects them but because they injure the common good. It is clear that no vision of the common good is possible if it is not a moral vision as well.

Matt Cooper goes on to ask: 'Is he [Dr Connell] suggesting that somehow non-Catholics in the legislature and the media do not have moral values which inform their views on issues like tax evasion and rape?'[10] Obviously, Matt Cooper has misunderstood the archbishop. There cannot be anything at the core of authentic Catholic moral teaching which does not at the same time accord with the deepest resonances of the human heart, and therefore with what serves the common good of all people. Anyone who seeks the common good is seeking the same things as Christians who see in Jesus the ultimate standard of truth and freedom, and, who is, for them, 'the way, truth and life'.[11]

Points of intersection
There is much reporting in newspapers and television which appeals to very basic instincts in us. We might not be very proud of the fact but we do take some pleasure in learning the often sordid details of other people's lives, their love affairs, their business scams. We like to see important people being taken down a peg or two. We have to take responsibility for the fact that this kind of journalism survives. In real terms, however, this kind of journalism makes money, but little impact.

There is another kind of journalism. It is the kind that somehow manages to reflect what Brendan Kennelly calls 'life's transcendent dignity'. As an example I have in mind Fergal Keane's letter to his newly-born son Daniel.[12] We can picture Keane, sitting at his typewriter, quietly picking out the keys with one hand as Daniel rests secure in his arms. As he looks at this sleeping child he is filled with a sense of the majesty of life, but also of its fragility. He has never felt more alive and more potent than he does at this moment. At the same time he recognises how much of what he valued in life until now – prizes, tributes, glory – have no meaning whatsoever. Staring into the face of this new life he dies to these. He recalls the faces of other children whose brief lives briefly intersected with his in places like Angola, Afghanistan and Rwanda. Significantly he recalls them by name. They are dead, victims largely of human neglect. These memories fill him with a great sense of protectiveness towards Daniel. Then he recalls his own birth and the story of love and love gone wrong in the life of his own alcoholic father. This is now part of Daniel's story too. He hoped that his father 'could hear, across the infinity between the living and the dead, your proud statement of arrival. For if he could hear, he would recognise the distinct voice of family, the sound of hope and new beginnings that you and all your innocence and freshness have brought to the world'.[13]

Keane evokes in us a sense of the wonder of parenthood and the giftedness of life. At the same time we experience shame at our own negligence in the face of massive suffering and need, and a sense of loss as we recall relationships in our own lives which, for one reason or another, fell apart. Significantly, Keane's collection of articles is subtitled *Despatches from the Heart.* Heidegger drew our attention to the fact that recording something is first and foremost an activity of the heart, *cor, cordis*. In the best of journalism heart speaks to heart. We are moved. We are affected. We are not just in-formed, we are trans-formed.

The birth of Fergal Keane's son was a small event in itself, of little newsworthiness outside his family circle. But the significance of an event is not determined by how many columns it rates in a newspaper. Kavanagh highlights this in his poem, 'Epic'. He observes two farmers, stripped to the waist, armed with pitchforks and ready to kill each other over a half-rood of land. An unimportant episode in itself when compared with the grey clouds of war gathering over mainland Europe at that very moment. He writes:

> I inclined
> To lose my faith in Ballyrush and Gortin
> Till Homer's ghost came whispering to my mind
> He said: I made the Iliad from such
> A local row. Gods make their own importance.[14]

'Gods make their own importance'. Good journalism unearths the spark of divinity hidden in even the most ordinary story of human turmoil or triumph. This kind of journalism challenges Christianity. Christian faith must interpret the complexity of human experience. It must address the plenitude of our humanity, the joyful and sorrowful mysteries, as they are recorded by poets, artists and the media. When journalism reveals, for example, genuine injustice and exploitation, it is a challenge to the Christian community to preach justice and practise what it preaches. When it records profound human suffering, it is a cry to show how such suffering somehow speaks to us of the mystery of God.

It is only being realistic to acknowledge that today media set the agenda for Christianity. If we do not address the issues which they raise, we force Christians to live in two worlds which seem to have little in common with one another. Ultimately we risk the marginalisation of Christian faith.

At the same time, if we accept the Christian perspective, we have to admit that only God has all the facts regarding events affecting his creatures, and so only God can write the *definitive* record.

A treasure, but in clay jars

In the last few years the media have rightly examined the conscience of the Church. They have pointed to our hypocrisy and double standards. They have shown how we have not fully believed or practised what we have professed. They have highlighted how, individually, and at times as a community, we have behaved shamefully and irresponsibly.

A self-examination might reveal sins of omission which have escaped media attention but which may well be at the root of the more publicised failures. For example: the failure to develop and sustain a form of ministry which is life-giving for all in the Church, including ministers themselves; a half-hearted approach to liturgical renewal; the failure to educate people into an adult faith, often leaving them with childish and destructive notions of God which have needlessly filled them with fear and guilt; a failure to preach the demands of justice.

That the treasure we hold, to use Paul's phrase,[15] we hold in clay jars, is something we should have known only too well. It is something which has always been known to God. Sin and failure lie at the heart of the human story which God has taken to himself in the crucifixion of Jesus Christ. They lie at the heart of the story, but not at its end. The end is resurrection and new life.

The challenge now is: how do we learn from our weakness and failure? We begin by acknowledging fully to ourselves and to those who have been offended by the Church that wrong has been done, whether by individuals, or by those in authority. We must do everything to repair the damage not only as the law requires but as justice and love demand.

As a community we must then seek and celebrate forgiveness and healing. Forgiveness, as John Shea writes, is 'not magnanimously forgetting faults, but the uncovering of self-worth when it is crusted over with self-hatred'.[16] We know we have accepted forgiveness when we have a restored sense of our own dignity and a renewed confidence in ourselves because of God's confidence in us.

The failures of the Christian community cannot be allowed to hold it back from proclaiming the Good News. Nor can they simply be left behind or ignored. If responded to prayerfully and practically, however, they will result in a greater trust in the power of the crucified God at work even in human weakness.

We begin to communicate by listening

There are some practical steps which the Church here in Ireland needs to take if it is to communicate the Gospel effectively at the turn of this century.

Some are of the opinion now that the Irish Church has missed the boat with regard to pastoral renewal. What is now needed is a plan for basic evangelisation.[17] The first step in evangelisation, i.e. in proclaiming the Good News, is listening. This is acknowledged in *Evangelii nuntiandi* of Paul VI. It is also reflected in the very first words of Vatican II's decree on Divine Revelation: *'Hearing* the Word of God, with reverence'. This listening is *prior* to 'proclaiming it with faith'.[18]

What we listen to is the Word of God. It is the Word of God which lives in the scripture and tradition of the Christian community. But it is also the Word of God as it takes flesh in people's daily lives. This is how the Word of God remains alive, fresh and youthful. If we fail to listen to one or other presence of God's Word, we will not understand it at all. Nor will we move beyond words into action.

Listening is first and foremost an inner disposition. It demands humility – it means we have something to learn. It also requires a level of trust in ourselves and in those to whom we are listening. Listening also involves risk: we may well be changed by what we hear. But if we are afraid to take the risk of listening, then our faith is weak. The parable of the talents makes clear that fear is the opposite of faith. The man with the one talent is punished; he buried it in the ground 'because he was afraid'.[19] The others are rewarded not because they were successful, but because they took risks. Risk-taking is part and parcel of discipleship. Playing safe is not. People listen to what the media have to say. It is important that we listen as well. The media can help us to discern 'the joys and hopes, the anguish and sadness of our day'.[20]

Media education
In the past, the Church invested heavily in education. We still consider it important to be involved and influential in the running and management of schools. But young people today are more likely to be influenced by what they are taught through television and newspapers than in school.[21] We need to take account of this.

How do we convince people to live according to Christian values today? We will not do this by frightening them as perhaps we did in the past.[22] Nor will we be able to limit choices regarding belief and behaviour. The Internet and, soon, digital television mean that even the state is unable to control what people see or read, even if it so wished. The main contribution the Church can make at this moment, therefore, is to educate people in how to make responsible choices. We need to concentrate on helping people to be free and mature enough in themselves that they can choose that which most accords with human dignity and well-being.

Specifically with regard to the media, the credibility of the Christian community depends on educated and articulate lay people confidently discussing matters of faith on the airwaves and in the newspaper columns. Again, Church leaders need to learn to trust lay people. They also have to accept that ageing black and white clerics, before they open their mouths at all, are likely to send many people reaching for the remote control.

Christian media

There is room for specifically Church-based media which provide forums for discussion of and education in issues primarily of interest to the Christian community. One of the great failures of the post-Vatican II Church is adult religious education. This could still be made good with effective use of modern means of communication. At the same time these media should not be inward-looking or incestuous, ecclesiastical equivalents of *Pravda*. Instead, they should create a genuine conversation between Christian faith and the issues and events which affect people's daily lives.

To make an important theological point: Church-based

media could play an important role both in the reception and development of Church teaching. How much of Vatican II's teaching has actually been received? How many people know more than the externals? No matter how many catechisms have been sold, people still need a forum in which to question and learn so that they might understand and believe.

Church-based media can also fulfil an important function with regard to the development of doctrine. This will be possible, however, only if conflicting views are allowed to be heard, and if the risk is taken of saying or believing the wrong thing. Open, frank and intelligent discussion has never damaged the faith, and attempts to stifle discussion usually do not work anyway. Disagreement and even dissent can play important roles in the life of the Church. Criticism needs to be given voice, and the key question is not if it is 'loyal' but whether or not it is justified. The wheat will always eventually be separated from the darnel. And the best way to prevent people from mistaking one for the other is by educating them.

There is a danger that Church-sponsored media might fall into the hands of fundamentalists. Fundamentalism is even more dangerous to faith than relativism or pluralism because it wears the apparel of orthodoxy. It provides quick-fix answers which temporarily assuage the pain of questioning but ultimately leaves faith hungry and undernourished. As Newman said, 'mere inherited faith, in those who can have an intelligent faith, is, to say the least, dangerous and inconsistent'.[23]

At the same time, specifically Church-based media should not take the place of a Christian presence in the public media. There are many people who would never buy a Church-sponsored newspaper or tune in to a religious broadcasting station. In any case, it is important that journalists and broadcasters, specifically motivated by their faith, can become accepted and respected among their peers, where exacting professional standards apply.

Conclusion

As we end one millennium and begin another, the Church in many ways has come of age. The media have played an important if not always welcome role in this maturation process. In an adult Church (and adult society) the only kind of authority which can be exercised with any degree of effectiveness is the authority of the truth. It was the only kind of authority which Jesus Christ claimed.

The Church now faces two challenges: to present the message of the Gospel in such a way that its promise of fulfilment is self-evident, and to educate people so that they can discern the truth in freedom. Both of these can only be accomplished by a vibrant and confident faith-community. The restoration of our confidence is dependent upon our trusting fully in the One who said:

> For as the rain and the snow come down from heaven,
> and do not return there until they have watered the
> earth, making it bring forth and sprout,
> giving seed to the sower and bread to the eater,
> so shall my word be that goes out from my mouth;
> it shall not return to me empty,
> but it shall accomplish that which I purpose,
> and succeed in the thing for which I sent it.[24]

Notes
1.   1 Cor 2:9.
2.   Ex 3:14.

3.   *Preface of Christmas* 1.

4.   Cf. *Dei verbum,* Prologue.

5.   'The story of Jesus ... is the human story in its full extent, from God to God, expanding our story that is only from womb to tomb.... This story does not happen in a privileged world in which it slips from earth to heaven as in a suction tube. It intersects with our story in all the latter's inconclusiveness and bitterness and expands it to its deific statute' (Sebastian Moore, 'Four steps towards making sense of theology', *The Downside Review,* 3, 1993, pp. 81, 82).

6.   'We do not live to ourselves, and we do not die to ourselves. If we live, we live to the Lord, and if we die, we die to the Lord; so then, whether we live or whether we die, we are the Lord's. For to this end Christ died and lived again, so that he might be Lord of both the dead and the living' (Rm 14:7-9).

7.   Cf. Lk 19:1-10; Jn 4:10-30; Jn 18:33-38.

8.   Jn 8:32.

9.   Cf., for example, Lk 13:12.

10. 'Religion and Media: A National Editor's Outlook', in this volume, p. 40ff.

11. Jn 14:6.

12. Fergal Keane, *Letter to Daniel – Despatches from the Heart,* London: Penguin, 1996, pp. 35-39.

13. *Letter to Daniel,* p. 38.

14. Patrick Kavanagh, *The Complete Poems,* Newbridge: Goldsmith Press, 1972, p. 238.

15. 2 Cor 7.

16. John Shea, *The Challenge of Jesus,* Texas: Thomas More Publishing, 1996, p. 128.

17. This view was expressed at a meeting of diocesan

representatives with the Bishops' National Millennium Planning Committee in December 1996.

18. 'Hearing the Word of God with reverence and proclaiming it with faith, the sacred Synod takes its direction from these words of St John: "We announce to you the eternal life which dwelt with the Father and was made visible to us. What we have seen and heard we announce to you, so that you may have fellowship with us and our common fellowship be with the Father and his Son Jesus Christ" (1 Jn 1:2-3). Therefore, following in the footsteps of the Council of Trent and of the First Vatican Council, the present Council wishes to set forth authentic doctrine on divine revelation and how it is handed on, so that by hearing the message of salvation the whole world may believe, by believing it may hope, and by hoping it may love' (*Dei verbum*, Prologue).

19. Mt 25:14-30.

20. John Paul II, *Redemptor hominis*.

21. 'The moral life of a community is determined, in part, by the images available to it for the formation of the imagination by which it lives. Artists and what we now call "the media" are primary providers of those images in the contemporary world.... Since the electronic "media" are a new and powerful technology without precedent in human experience, there is no body of traditional wisdom by which we can understand and assess their effects on the formation of people, communities, democracies – or a global commons'. Laurent A. Parks *et al., Common fire – lives of commitment in a complex world,* Boston: Beacon Press, 1996, pp. 229, 231.

22. It is extraordinary to think that people were encouraged to behave morally out of fear when one recalls the statement by St Thomas Aquinas, 'He therefore who avoids evil not because it is evil but because of the command of God is not free, but he who avoids evil because it is evil is free' (Commentary on 2 Cor 3, quoted in Vincent McNamara, *The Truth in Love,* Dublin: Gill & Macmillan, 1988, p. 42).

23. Quoted before the preface in Michael Paul Gallagher, *Help my unbelief,* Dublin: Veritas, 1983.

24. Is 55:10-12.

THE CONTRIBUTORS

Vincent Browne, journalist and broadcaster, recently qualified as a barrister.

Eamonn Conway, a priest of the Tuam diocese, is a theologian at All Hallows College.

Matt Cooper is the Editor of *The Sunday Tribune*.

John Cunningham is the Editor of *The Connacht Tribune*.

Cardinal Cahal B. Daly, Archbishop Emeritus of Armagh, is the author of many books on issues of justice and peace and on the peace process in Northen Ireland.

Thomas Flynn is Bishop of Achonry and former spokesman for the Irish Bishops' Conference.

Liz Gibson Harries is Press Officer for the Church of Ireland.

Kevin Hegarty, a priest of the Killala diocese, is Editor of *Céide* and a former Editor of *Intercom*.

Pat Heneghan is the Managing Director of Heneghan Public Relations.

Colm Kilcoyne, a priest of the Tuam diocese, is a journalist.

Joe Little is Religious Affairs Correspondent, RTÉ.

Oliver Maloney is a former Director-General of RTÉ.

Dermod McCarthy, a priest of the Dublin diocese, is Editor of Religious Programmes, RTÉ, and Chairman of the EBU Religious Broadcasting Committee.

Dermot Mullane is Executive Editor, RTÉ News.

Helena O'Donoghue RSM is the Provincial Leader of the South-Central Province of the Sisters of Mercy.

Andy Pollak, former Religious Affairs Correspondent for *The Irish Times*, is now its Education Correspondent.

David Quinn is a columnist for *The Sunday Times* and Editor of *The Irish Catholic*.

All Hallows College was founded in 1842 as a seminary. Today it continues to be a vibrant centre for renewal and development in the Church, attracting students not only from all parts of Ireland but also from overseas. It has a student body of over three hundred, school-leavers as well as mature students, drawn from all walks of life. The College awards diplomas and degrees up to doctoral level under the auspices of the National Council for Educational Awards. It is responsible to the Vatican Congregation for the Evangelisation of Peoples.

The Continuing Education Department at All Hallows College offers people already engaged in the Church's mission and in various ministries an opportunity to respond to personal and professional needs. Programmes address the issues of the day but also look towards the mission and ministry of the Church into the next millennium. Recognising that God and the human are always found together, courses endeavour to facilitate theological reflection in a manner which also promotes personal growth.

Among the programmes in Continuing Education currently offered by the College are: Preparing for Ministries, which involves one night a week for two years and aims at personal growth in Christian faith and renewal of parish life; Renewal for Ministry, a short sabbatical course which offers experienced ministers an opportunity for study, reflection and updating; the annual Summer School, which consists of a number of one-week courses and conferences which meet specific needs as they emerge in the life of the Christian community. The papers published here are the proceedings of one of these conferences.